BlackJack: The Real Deal

BLACKJACK:

The Real Deal

By

J. Phillip Vogel

A RavenHaus Publishing Book

New Jersey

BlackJack: The Real Deal

Edited by Karrie Zukowski

Cover designed by Lori Vogel

Cover photo by Gail Hannagan

RavenHaus Publishing

2 Fox Hill Rd

Califon, NJ 07830

RavenHaus Books on the World Wide Web:

http://www.ravenhauspublishing.com

ISBN: 0-9659845-0-8

Library of Congress Catalog Number: 97-092731

First edition: November 1997

Printed in the United States of America

0 9 8 7 6 5 4 3 2 1

To my parents,

Dr. Jerome Vogel and Dolores Vogel, thank you.

PREFACE

This is a book about casino Blackjack. Its purpose is to better prepare the novice and the intermediate player for casino gambling. I will explore the basic rules and strategies of Blackjack, as well as the best tool for the casino gambler: card-counting. If you think you're a good player, a strong contender against the casino, and you don't know basic strategy and card-counting methods, you're only fooling yourself. I'm not guaranteeing that everyone who reads this book will win. I am saying that those who truly want to win, and who read and memorize basic strategy, and the simplified versions of card-counting contained in this book, will be on the right road to winning. Without that knowledge, you are your own enemy, and the casino's best friend.

I'll show you everything you need to know about Blackjack, from when to take a seat, to when to take a walk. The strategy utilized in this book involves self-control, timing, a little mathematics and a strong desire to win, not to just play.

Do you want to beat the casino at its own game?

Then do it.

TABLE OF CONTENTS

1. INTRODUCTION

1.1 WHAT IS A GAMBLER?

A gambler is a different sort of person. He thrives on the excitement of the game, whatever the game may be. It's the thrill of the risk, the randomness of each turn of a card, or roll of the dice that is the lure. These things are an integral part in all who venture into the casino, but what is the underlying aspect to all gambling? Making money! All gamblers have a strong desire to win money. To win you have to venture beyond the mere thrill of the game. You have to understand all aspects of Blackjack. You have to have a strategy, a complete knowledge of the game, and have to be able to make logical plays. In short, you have to be perfect.

This book discusses Blackjack, one of the most popular and profitable casino games. Unfortunately, most of the profit for this game ends up in the pocket of the casino, due to the lack of knowledge and skill by the player. This book will help change all that. I'm going to talk about every aspect of the game, from the buy-in, to basic card-counting. We'll discuss the table, the odds, and the strategies that you'll need to be a winner in Blackjack. While I can't guarantee everyone will be successful with this program, I can tell you that by utilizing these strategies you give yourself the ammunition to go into battle against the big boys, the casino, and hopefully come out a winner. In the end, though, it's up to you.

1.2 THE SUCCESSFUL SIX

Before I jump into all of the strategies and rules that you need to know, there is something I must discuss that is so important, that all else must take a back seat. That something is your "equipment".

To gamble, you must know about the game. To gamble successfully, you must have the right "equipment". To put it simply, these are:

1. Proper Bankroll
2. Knowledge
3. Betting Strategy
4. Self Control
5. Understanding Probability and Trends
6. Patience

These are your resources, the lifeblood of the gambler. If you are without any ONE of them, your chances of winning fall drastically. If you are not perfect with each of them, you will lose. Throughout the book, I discuss each of these subjects in depth, but for now I'd like to give you a brief overview of the successful six.

PROPER BANKROLL: No scared money. Flat out, that's the rule. Your bankroll is your source of competition, and without it, you're going nowhere. The amount of money you bring to the table is directly proportional to the amount you can expect to win. Don't ever expect to go into a casino with $50 and come out with $5,000. Get over it, it won't happen. The rule of thumb is simply this: Bring 40 times the amount of your initial bet.

KNOWLEDGE: You must know the game. Every aspect of it. From the rules to the odds. There is no way you can compete successfully against the casino and not know everything. It's simply a must. Don't be scared by this. It's not as hard as you think, and this book will cover everything.

BETTING STRATEGY: You must have a game plan. Contrary to popular belief, gambling is not solely up to chance. There are strategies that must be followed; predetermined betting styles and amounts, all of which are based on your bankroll. These methods will help you to minimize your loses, *and* take advantage of streaks.

SELF-CONTROL: Determines how well you can handle yourself in the casinos, especially when things are not going your way. Self-control is the ability to walk away when you should, even though you don't want to. It is the power to make certain wagers and decisions that might scare you. It is the power to stand on a 12, or to split 8's against a king. It is the power to become a winner. If you're a gambler and you lack self-control, you'll be out of the business pretty damn quick.

UNDERSTANDING PROBABILITY AND TRENDS: You must know the chances involved in any decision. Every game in a casino is governed by rules of probability. To make the most of your bankroll, you need to play only those games (as well as the side wagers within those games) that have the best odds of turning a profit.

PATIENCE: This is the mark of a professional. Never lose your cool, and never try to rush a win. If you're down $50, don't try to get it all back in one play. It will eat your money faster than you can ever imagine. Your patience will pay off, but you have to be ready to wait, not to play.

These are the SUCCESSFUL SIX, and they are the basics of what you need to be a winner. If you implement these six, and incorporate them into the methods that I will teach you in this book, you'll drastically increase your chances of beating the casino at its own game.

1.3 VIGORISH: THE CASINO'S HAMMER

Vigorish. If you're going to gamble, then you are going to hear this word. Once you understand what it is, you'll understand how a casino stays in business. You'll also learn which games to stay away from and which ones to play.

Vigorish is the edge the casino has in its favor for any game. For example, in Roulette, a single number bet pays 35 to 1. But there are 36 numbers, as well as one zero, and one double zero. That gives a total of 38 numbers. So let's say you pick your favorite number, lucky 7, and bet $10 on it. If it hits, you win $350, a great payoff right? Not really. Since there are actually 38 numbers, including the 0, and 00, and you bet on one of them, you have a 1 in 38 chance of winning, or 37 to 1 odds. But as I said, the casino only pays 35 to 1, a vigorish of about 5.26%. That vigorish is how the casino ensures itself a profit.

So what can you do, if the payouts are always going to be lower than the odds really are? For starters, you should only play games, and make wagers that have the highest percentage of winning, or the lowest vigorish. For example, when you know basic strategy in Blackjack, the vigorish is only about 1.41%. That's a big difference from most of the other games, and wagers in a casino, where the vigorish is routinely 5% or higher.

By playing those games with the lowest vigorish, you reduce the profit for the casino, and in turn increase your odds of being a winner. Here's a quick, little hint for you players who want to watch out for high vigorish wagers: whenever you hear casino personnel talking to the players, reminding them to take certain bets - that's a no-no.

For example, in Craps, often you'll hear the dealers "reminding" the players to get their "any seven" bet in, or other proposition bets before it's too late. Do you think that's to be nice? Think again. The house vigorish on those bets is incredibly high. The "any seven" bet carries a 16.67% vigorish on it, and many other "prop" bets are over 11%. Those are bad bets, but people do them. Some people even love them, and will bet them every second. The sad part is, they don't even know how bad those bets are.

1.4 COMMON BLACKJACK TERMS

1. **Anchorman**: Refers to the player seated closest to the dealer's right.
2. **Blackjack**: Also known as "21", it is both the name and object of the game. It also refers to a player's original 2 cards, when those cards consist of an ace, and a 10-value card.
3. **Breaking**: Drawing cards to a hand so that its total exceeds 21.
4. **Burn Card**: After the shuffle, a common practice in casinos is to discard the top card of the new shoe, before the deal begins.
5. **Card-counting**: Refers to the action of keeping a mental record of the cards played within a shoe.
6. **Chasing**: Chasing is when a player tries to recoup previous loses. It usually results in further losses.
7. **Check-change**: A term used by the dealers in communication with a pit boss when exchanging a player's money for chips.
8. **Chips**: These are the tokens used by casinos in place of currency. They vary from casino to casino.
9. **Color In**: This refers to the exchange of multiple low value chips for fewer, higher denomination chips. For

example, you ask the dealer to "color in" 20, $5 chips, for 1, $100 chip.

10. **Dealer**: The casino employee in charge of the Blackjack game.
11. **Deck**: The standard pack of playing cards, consisting of 13 variation of four suits, a total of 52 cards.
12. **Double Down**: The term for increasing your initial wager based on the next turn of the cards. Only one more card is allowed when you double down.
13. **Draw**: To take a card.
14. **First Base**: The seat closest to the dealers left, and the first player to receive a card.
15. **Good Shoe**: A winning round consisting of all decks between shuffles.
16. **Hand**: The cards dealt to the players.
17. **Hard Total**: A hand consisting of no aces.
18. **Hit**: To draw more cards.
19. **Hole Card**: The dealer's unseen card.
20. **Insurance**: A side bet made during normal play when the dealer's upcard is an ace. The bet wins if the dealer has Blackjack and pays 2:1.
21. **Multiple Deck**: A Blackjack game where more than one deck is used.

22. **Push:** A tie between the player and the dealer. No money is exchanged.
23. **Shoe**: A device used to facilitate an easier deal with multiple decks of cards. It is also the term for the sum of all hands between shuffles.
24. **Shuffle**: The mixing of cards by the dealer at the end of a shoe.
25. **Single Deck Game**: A game in which only one deck of cards is used.
26. **Soft Total**: A hand consisting of at least one ace, which is counted as 1.
27. **Splitting**: The action of separating a pair of numerically identical cards, and playing two hands from them.
28. **Standing**: Taking no more cards.
29. **Stiff**: A bad hand that must be drawn to, such as 12-16.
30. **Third Base**: The anchorman.
31. **Tip/Toke**: A gratuity to or bet for the dealer by the player.
32. **Upcard**: The exposed card of the dealer's hand.

2. BANKROLL

2.1 THE AMMUNITION

There are many things necessary to be a successful gambler, and there is not one thing that ranks number 1. But just as surely as I'm a gambler, bankroll is among the most important. To a gambler a bankroll decides what, when and how long you can play. If you don't have the money, you don't get the action. But why is it so important?

All gambling is based on probability and statistics, and all winning is based on trends and bankroll. The statistics tells you that something must happen. Probability tells you that it must happen during a certain period of time. Trends work to balance these two together and bankroll determines if the player will reach a favorable trend.

Bankroll also tells the player what he can bet, and what games he can play. A player with a fifty-dollar bankroll can't expect to go to a casino and play $10 slot machines, no matter how much he likes them. At best, he could play on the 25-cent machines. If you don't like that, get a bigger bankroll. If you can't, don't gamble. You'll lose every cent you have.

Later, I'm going to be talking about percentage, how much you can bet, how much you should expect to win, and the absolute most you should except as a loss. All of these things are tuned into your bankroll, and the smaller the bankroll, the less of a profit you can expect to receive. For now, just know that the rule of thumb for the Blackjack player is to bring forty times the amount of your initial wager. So, if you're at a $5 table, you need to bring about $200. I know that to some of you out there, $200 is nothing. To some people however, that can be a lot of money to risk for a few hours gambling.

For those people, I have included in this book betting strategies that may help to keep you in the game longer, and hopefully finish with a profit. If you're playing with only a little money, called a scared bankroll, you may be afraid to make the bets that are required, and you'll only end up hurting yourself in the long run. I strongly urge everyone with a short bankroll to wait a little bit longer, save up the extra money, and don't go to the casino until you have a bankroll large enough to turn you a profit.

2.2 EXPECTATION

Every person who enters a casino not only hopes to win, but downright expects it. If they didn't, they probably wouldn't go. (Who would go expecting to lose?) But the majority of the people do not bring the right amount of money in order to complete. They break rule number one of the Successful Six: proper bankroll. It's this money that decides how much you can realistically hope to win.

I told you earlier that you need about 40 times the amount of the initial wager in order to compete successfully. If the minimum bet is $5, then your bankroll should be $200, and not one penny less. This is not optional, it is a necessity. Without the proper bankroll you'll play scared, and playing scared is the same as playing bad. You lose your strategy, your self-control and your patience. You'll begin to get nervous and make the wrong plays. In short, you'll wipe yourself out.

I've mentioned that the bankroll, among its other jobs, determines how much you can expect to win. This is true. Your bankroll alone determines expectation. So, on a $200 bankroll how much can you expect to win? Realistically, about $60. That's about 30% of your bankroll, and this is called a profit expectation. This percentage should be based on your starting capital and always be decided upon before you even begin playing. If you don't want to win a mere $60, then bring more money. It's that simple. Profit expectations do not have to be 30%, but they should be set at a comfortable, logical amount, anywhere from 10-40%.

2.3 LOSING MONEY

Just as there are logical amounts that you can expect to win, there are also limits to the amount of money that you should be willing to lose. In a casino, every penny counts, and I don't want you to throw away one cent, even of it's the last chip you have. Even if it's a dollar, it's important. Remember that.

Have you ever put your last $10 up on one bet, because you think, "Oh, what the hell, I've lost this much, ten bucks is not gonna make much difference." If you said no, I'm impressed. At some time or another, almost everyone has done it. But why do I think that's such a bad thing? Because you should never have let it get that far. Why are you down all the way to your last $10? You should have set a limit to the amount you are willing to lose.

To many of you, that sounds easy enough, but in reality it is one of the most difficult things in the world to do: to leave the casino losing, while you still have money in your pocket. Think about it, you're down $100, but you still have $100 left, just sitting there in your pocket, all ready to go. You could use that money to try to win back what you lost. And why not? That money was earmarked for gambling anyway, right? Big mistake.

Knowing when enough is enough is hard. Having the self-control to set an amount that you will accept as a loss and to walk away when you reach that amount can really hurt. But it's necessary. This will keep you from being totally destroyed, and is paramount to being a winning gambler. Remember, no one can win 100% of the time. It almost impossible to win 70%, so don't let the losses set you back so hard that your future wins can't balance it out. Don't feel bad about losing $100 in a casino, if you went with $300. Sure, it's not any fun, but it sure as hell beats being down the whole $300!

So how much should I allow myself to lose? That depends upon personal preference. I would suggest about 40-50%, but no higher. If you go with $200, and you're down $100, that's it, close up shop and bag it for the day. You're fighting a losing battle, and no matter what you do, you're probably going to just lose more. It happens. Take the rest of the money, and put it towards the start of your next bankroll. You're already halfway there.

2.4 BANKROLL MANAGEMENT: SESSION, GOALS, AND LIMITS

What I'm going to do now is give you a strategy for money management that I want you to follow. It's very simple, so simple, in fact, that the hardest part will not be in remembering how to do it, but rather in getting you to break your old habits.

The first thing I want you do to is to break down the sum of your money into sessions. I would suggest a minimum of three. So if you come to the casino with $300, you break that amount down to three sessions of $100 each. Now the important thing to remember here is, your bankroll, the determining factor for how you are going to bet is no longer considered $300, but $100, because that's the total amount that you have to wager with for this session. Ideally, to play Blackjack, you should have 40 times your initial bet. In Atlantic City, where the table minimums are $5, that would require you to have $600, a total of $200 per session. To some people that's just flat out of reach. But this is the figure you should have to compete.

Now these sessions should be, in your mind at least, considered three separate trips to the casino. The amount of money in your bankroll *becomes the amount of the individual sessions.* So that the $300 you brought with you is really only $100 for the duration of any session. You may not touch the other money until you have finished your session. Once you have finished a session, you then place the remainder of the money elsewhere, never to be touched again. That ensures that you will not leave the casino totally wiped out.

Now as you are playing in a session, you will have two guidelines by which to follow: a goal and a limit. As I have already discussed, these are set prior to entering the casino, because they are based on the total sum of money that you have brought with you, your bankroll.

Your goal is the amount of money that you would like to win, based solely on your session bankroll. For instance, if you are at a table with $100, and you've set a goal of winning 30% of that, you are trying to win a total of $30. Once you reach that amount, you have reached your goal. Do you stop playing? No way! You could be in the middle of a hot trend, and to call it quits when you reached your 30% would be ludicrous. Instead, your next move is to break that amount - that $30 - down even further into "mini-sessions". In a mini-session, your object is to try to win above you percentage goal, without risking your original bankroll.

What you do is break the 30% in half, and play only with one of those halves. In this instance, you'd be playing with a total of $15. When that money is gone, that's when you call it quits for that session, and move on to your next bankroll, while still retaining a 15% win in the previous session. By doing that you are guaranteeing yourself a win for that round of play. It's simply a lot of self-control, and an intelligent use of your money.

By breaking that money down into mini-sessions, you're allowing yourself the freedom to play further, and possibly turn that 15% into a windfall, while at the same time restricting yourself from losing what you've already won. Make sense?

2.5 LIMITATIONS

Now you understand what sessions are, and while during a winning session how to secure yourself a profit. Now let's turn full circle and examine what to do to prevent you from being totally wiped out. Limits.

I mentioned earlier in this book about limits, and how you use them to protect the bulk of your bankroll. They are not based on your bankroll, like your goals are, but rather what you are "comfortable" in losing. Now I understand that you are never comfortable losing money, but I mean a figure that won't kill you to lose. For me, that's about 30-50%. Anything beyond that, and I have the distinct desire to hang myself. Any of you out there who have gone to a casino and been wiped out will know this feeling. It sinks all the way down to the bottom of your stomach and eats you from the inside out.

If I go into a casino with $300, and come out with $150, I'm a hell of a lot more relaxed then if I lost my entire roll of $300. Sure I lost a decent sum of money, but I'm not broke, and I have the beginning of another bankroll. The casinos won't be leaving anytime too soon, so I'll always have another chance to win that money back.

That's why I set a limit, before I ever enter the casino, to how much I'll lose. It's not truly based on my bankroll, rather it's a percentage guideline that I use to protect my money. If my total bankroll is $50 or $500, I'll still have a limit of 50% of the total. If the casino takes that 50%, that's it, I'm done for the day. No trying to win it back then and there. In my experience, more often then not you lose even more.

One final note in all this: the limit is based on the total bankroll, and that, therefore transfers over to your sessions. If you have a $300 bankroll, that's $100 per session, and a loss limit of $50 per session. If you lose that $50, that session is over, and the remaining money is put away, never to be touched again. If you want to continue playing, you have to start a new session, with another $100.

I know this may seem a little ridiculous, changing money with yourself, and breaking it up into sessions, but it keeps you under control, and lets you keep track of your money more easily. It lets you see exactly where your money is going, and can help to slow your pace down. It's a very easy thing to lose $100 in a casino in a short while. By breaking that money down you can slow the pace, make you take stock of your current situation, and maybe get you off of that "bad" table that you're at. You'll see that you're at an end of a session, and since that table wasn't any good, you won't dump another wad of session money into it. It helps to control your impulses, and therefore your money.

2.6 SYNOPSIS

So what are the important points that I have discussed in regard to your bankroll. If you can't name them right off the top of your head, go back and re-read the last section. They are that important. In a nutshell, however, they are:

1. Bring the proper bankroll amount, 40 times the initial bet.
2. Set profit expectation amount, i.e., what you can logically expect to win, based on your bankroll.
3. Set a maximum amount of money that you are willing to lose, and never exceed that amount.
4. Recognize that all wagering in the casino is based entirely on your starting capital.

Of course, some of you won't listen to these rules, but I think that many of you, especially those of you who are tired of losing your money, will take this advice to heart. You'll realize the truth of what I'm saying and will actively try to incorporate these teachings into your gambling style.

For those of you who don't agree with these ideas so far, I hope that by the end of this book, I can change your mind. Bankroll is so important to gambling, and the reason for gambling is to win. And you can't win without following the rules to bankroll management.

3. KNOW THE GAME

3.1 THE BASICS

To begin with, let's briefly consider the game of Blackjack. In Blackjack, the object of the game is to try to get a total score of twenty-one, or closer to twenty-one then the house without going over. Sounds easy? Well believe me, it's not. There is a strategy to Blackjack that must be followed to the letter if you are to stand even a slim chance of leaving that casino with more money in your pocket than you came with. Without this strategy, you're giving about a 40% edge in favor of the house. That's one hell of an advantage. And believe me, millions of people every year enter the casinos ignorantly handing over this 40% edge, seemingly unaware that you can reduce that number to a mere 1.41%. That's a big difference, and some of the best odds in a casino.

How do you do it. You memorize the basic strategy tables, like those included in this book. With these, you will always know the best statistical options available to you for any variation of cards that you might see. If that sounds imposing, then good. This is a tough game, and there is a lot to know. For now, though we're going to start off easy, and go over the basics of the game and get to the real meat and potatoes of Blackjack later.

3.2 THE LAYOUT OF THE TABLE

To many of you, the game of Blackjack is entirely new. Whether this is your first experience with gambling or just your first time at the tables, there are some general features that you need to know. To you others who already know this part, feel free to skip this chapter. (But don't get into the habit of skipping around: you may miss some important stuff!)

Basically, the Blackjack table is a slightly modified oval, with clearly marked areas for where to place your wager. The number of players per table is around seven, (it varies depending upon where you play) and there are seats for each player. The dealer sits opposite you, in the pit, and deals in order from his left. Directly in front of the dealer is a chip rack, containing the casino's seemingly endless bankroll. To the dealers left, away from the players is a box, called a shoe, from which the dealer draws the cards for play. Since most games you will encounter are multiple deck games, up to about eight decks, the shoe facilitates an easier draw of the cards for the dealer. A shoe is also a term for the sum of the rounds of play of all of the cards contained within this box. So, a "new shoe" refers to the time right after the shuffle, and just prior to the dealing of the initial hand. To buy into a game, you merely place the money in front of you towards the dealer either after a hand or prior to the beginning of a new shoe. The dealer will pick up the money, count it, announce the total to the pit boss, and exchange the dollars for chips of equal value. Always count your chips after receiving them, for while it is rare, the dealers are human and may make mistakes. If such a mistake does occur, notify the dealer immediately, or you may lose that money.

All tables specify the maximum and minimum wagers allowed per hand. In Atlantic City, the minimum is $5 per hand. While to some of you that amount may seem small, to others, those with the small bankrolls, that may seem high priced. But the casinos don't care. You want to play, you have to meet the minimum. The table itself states some of the basic rules and payoffs of the game. Commonly, this just says "Dealer must draw to 16, and stand on all 17s", "Insurance pays 2-1", and "Blackjack pays 3-2". As I said, these are the very basics and there is a lot more to Blackjack than that. But I will get into that later.

3.3 SITTING DOWN

When you first approach a table that meets your bankroll, for example, a $5 table, you may take any available seat, and if no one is there, play will begin when you sit down. The table does not have to have any more than one player at it for it to open. As I said, you may take any available seat, and where you sit depends upon personal preference. The first chair, closest to the dealer's left, and the first player to be dealt cards is commonly called first base, and the last player, on the dealer's immediate right, called the anchorman.

Your own personal preference and availability determine where you sit, but the professional usually prefers the anchorman position, or the one to the dealer's immediate right. The reason for this is basically because they can get a total view of all of the cards currently out, and they can then get a slight advantage in knowing what decisions to make. This is especially helpful with the card-counter, who then gets an even better count of the current cards, and has more time to make a decision. I must caution you, however, for a novice, this seat probably isn't the best choice, because your decisions may help or hurt the outcome of the hands. I can't count the number of times I've seen a novice cost the table a win because of a bad decision, like taking a hit on a thirteen versus a dealer's 5 or a 6. Believe me, most people at the tables are not shy when you cost them a bet through bad play, and the novice quickly finds himself unwelcome.

To be fair however, another reason the novice should not sit at that spot is because of the number of bad players right alongside them. (Unfortunately, most of *them*, think of themselves as regular pros). These people routinely blame the anchorman for their losses even though the move you made was correct, but the dealer won anyway. But after you have learned and memorized the information in this book, and other books in this series, such as advanced card-counting, take that position as often as you can. Your knowledge will save you and the table more often then it will cost it. And besides that, why be at the mercy of the bad player who doesn't know basic strategy or card-counting, when you can be in control of the hand?

3.4 PROBABILITY VERSUS TRENDS

Before I begin discussing all of the intricacies of basic strategy, I'd first like to mention to you the concepts of probability and trends. As many of you know, probability is simply the likelihood of a random event happening. A tossing coin will land on heads 50% of the time. That's the probability of the happening. In Blackjack, certain hands have a high likelihood of success, like a "20", while others do not, like a "16". These are concepts that are familiar to you.

Contained within the section of basic strategy, I have included many of the statistical chances of being dealt certain cards when you have a particular hand. So I will not mention those here. What I am mainly concerned with is discussing the controversial topic of trends. Point blank -- they do exist. I don't care who tells you otherwise, if you've ever been in a casino, then you know what I'm talking about. You've seen them. You've watched while the dealer has won 25 hands in a row, or maybe you yourself have been dealt that many winning hands in a row. Personally, the most winning hands I have ever been dealt, in a row, was 17. Did I clean up? Yes! I recognized the trend as it was happening, and bet accordingly. And therein lies one of the greatest problems of gambling, recognizing a trend.

In all honesty, you can never "see" the trend until it is finished. You never know if you will win 5 hands, 3 hands or 50 hands. You will only know after the streak is finished. And if you're like most people, you'll be kicking yourself for not taking advantage of it.

Now, what causes a streak is in debate, but simply put all things have a probability of occurring, while it is small, there is the probability that you will win 50 hands in a row. The key point in probability is that things have to balance out numerically. Tossing a coin is a 50-50 shot, but is it always heads-tails-heads-tails-heads-tails, etc.? No way. But in the long run, the number of heads, and the number of tails will balance out. That's just the way it is.

As a gambler, you want to be in on the "good" trends. That is, a series by which you win more money than the house. This is not as easy as it sounds. You need proper betting strategies, patience and the control to make the proper types of wagers. You can't just rely on the "luck of the draw" and try to ride with a trend. You, the player, are partially responsible for creating the trend. Your knowledge of whether to take a hit or stand, when to split, or when to double down all work to create the trend. You can't just play blindly.

I'll go into the discussion of trends later, but for now I wanted you to understand what they are, and to realize that they can be a driving force in not only gambling, but also winning.

3.5 BASIC STRATEGY: WHAT YOU MUST KNOW!!!

The following is a series of charts and tables that you must memorize before you even enter the casino. I cannot stress this fact enough. If you really want to win in a casino, to even have a chance you must memorize these tables. Every decision that you could possibly have to make is in these tables. By knowing this information you reduce the house vigorish against you to about 1.41%, making this one of the most winning games in the casino, but only if you know it!! Does it really make that big of a difference? You bet your ass it does. Without this you will lose. Maybe not every time, as anyone can have an occasional win, but frequently. Know it!!!

3.6 HARD TOTALS

In this book, hard totals refer to the combination of the first two cards that you are dealt, when not dealt at least one ace. However, we will not consider the totals of the two cards when the total is below twelve, such as a nine, because those hands follow other rules, and can be hit safely, with no fear of breaking. (Exceeding a total of 21.)

Whether you should take a hit or stand depends upon two related factors: the player's total and the dealer's upcard. These rules should always be obeyed (unless you are a card-counter) as they drastically increase your chances of winning. At first, some of these decisions may seem a little odd, or even just plain wrong, but bear in mind that these are proven methods based on probability and statistics, and without them, you'll just have to pray along with the rest of the future hall of fame losers.

TABLE I: HARD TOTAL STRATEGIES

Player's Upcard	Dealer's Upcard									
Total	2	3	4	5	6	7	8	9	10-K	A
11 OR LOWER	Hit	Hit	Hit	Hit	Hit	Hit	Hit	Hit	Hit	Hit
12	Hit	Hit	Stand	Stand	Stand	Hit	Hit	Hit	Hit	Hit
13	Stand	Stand	Stand	Stand	Stand	Hit	Hit	Hit	Hit	Hit
14	Stand	Stand	Stand	Stand	Stand	Hit	Hit	Hit	Hit	Hit
15	Stand	Stand	Stand	Stand	Stand	Hit	Hit	Hit	Hit	Hit
16	Stand	Stand	Stand	Stand	Stand	Hit	Hit	Hit	Hit	Hit
17-21	Stand	Stand	Stand	Stand	Stand	Stand	Stand	Stand	Stand	Stand

We hit all hands that range from a 12 through a 16 when the dealer shows a 7 because we have to assume the dealer's hole card is a facecard, and therefore already has at least 17. If we were to stand on one of those values we would expect to lose. Now it is not always the case that the dealer already has 17, but without card-counting there is no way to guess what his card is. Therefore, we must take a hit.

When the dealer is showing a 2-6, a bust card, the player must stand on whatever his or her total is, and hope that the dealer breaks. The exception to this is when the player has a 12, and the dealer has a 12 or 13. Why is this? Let's look at it from a statistical angle. How many cards can break you when you have a 12: 10, J, Q, and K. How many cards can work for you:

A, 2, 3, 4, 5, 6, 7, 8, and 9. That's a 9 to 4 advantage. Nine cards can help you, and only four can hurt you. Now, some of you are saying why take the chance at all of getting that facecard? Why not just hope the dealer breaks? For the same reason: only four cards can hurt him. I'd rather take advantage of the 9 to 4 odds that I would improve my hand than give it to the dealer. Sure, sometimes it will break me, but more often than not it will save me and perhaps the entire table.

You'll also notice in the table that we never hit a hard 17 or above, even if the dealer is showing an 8-A. The odds are too much against you pulling a breaking card, when the dealer might only have a stiff card underneath. I know I told you to always assume that the dealer has a face card underneath, and that with him showing an 8 against your 7, you're automatically losing. Well, unless you're playing Double Exposure (Blackjack where both of the dealer's cards are visible), you don't know what that card is. So why take a hit on 17, when only 4 cards could possibly help you and 9 could hurt you? The dealer might very well have another 8 underneath? Just don't do it. I know that some of you won't listen and will occasionally take a hit. As strange as it may seem to some of you, I have actually seen it happen. Not often, but I have seen it.

As a final note in this section, just remember never, ever take a hit from 12-16 when the dealer is showing a 4, 5 or 6. These are the worst possible upcards that the dealer could have as he has a very good chance of breaking.

Some of you will follow these hard total strategies to the letter, others never will. You who memorize these decisions will undoubtedly, eventually, clash with those who won't. And they will chastise you for what they, in their ignorance, see as a bad move. Stick to your guns. When they yell at you for taking a hit against the dealer's 12 versus your 12, they're only showing how poor a player they are, and the dealers, the pit boss, and the few, other good players will know it. Don't be intimidated by loud mouth jerks whose only sure bet in life is that they'll never be a real winner.

3.7 SOFT TOTALS

I've spoken with you about hard totals, and now we're going to discuss the soft totals. First of all, a soft total refers to any hand that contains an ace. For example, an ace and 6 is a soft seventeen, an ace and 4 is a soft fifteen, and etc. The ace is obviously being counted as an 11. The soft total works to the player's advantage in that he may increase his wager, which we will discuss later, and it affords some "breathing room" in what could otherwise have been a poor hand.

TABLE II: SOFT TOTALS

Player's Upcard	**Dealer's Upcard**									
Total	2	3	4	5	6	7	8	9	10-K	A
A2-A5	Hit	Hit	Hit	Db	Db	Hit	Hit	Hit	Hit	Hit
A6	Hit	Db	Db	Db	Db	Hit	Hit	Hit	Hit	Hit
A7	Stand	Db	Db	Db	Db	Stand	Stand	Hit	Hit	Stand
A8	Stand	Stand	Stand	Stand	Stand	Stand	Stand	Stand	Stand	Stand
A9	Stand	Stand	Stand	Stand	Stand	Stand	Stand	Stand	Stand	Stand
A-(10-K)	BJ	BJ	BJ	BJ	BJ	BJ	BJ	BJ	BJ	BJ
Hit = Take 1 card Stand = Take no further action Db = Double Down BJ = Blackjack, Stand										

In a nutshell, those are the rules you must follow when dealt a soft-total. By following those simple rules you are reducing the house vigorish and increasing your chances of winning. But anytime, and I mean anytime, you go against these set rules you hand money from your pocket back to the casino.

Now, some of these moves may seem controversial, and irrational. For example, why do you stand on a soft 18 when the dealer is showing a 2, 7, 8 or A, yet take a hit or double down during other instances? This is probably one of the most misplayed of all hands when in a casino due to lack of knowledge and strategy by the average player. Let's look at what's going on:

A7 versus 2: There are only 3 cards that can help your hand, A, 2 and 3; 4 cards that result in the same total, 10, J, Q and K, and 5 that would give you an even worse hand, 4, 5, 6, 7, 8 and 9. That leaves you with 5:3 ratio of bad to good cards, a bad bet when the dealer is showing a 2. Furthermore, if you do pull one of the remaining four cards that don't change your hand, the 10, J, Q or K, you are taking away the potential breaking card for the dealer if he has a face card underneath! So what you end up with is a statistical decrease in your odds or winning by taking a hit on a soft 18 when the dealer is showing a 2.

You stand on the soft 18 when the dealer shows a 7, because he has a potential 17, and your soft 18 will already beat him. Now I realize that I already mentioned that the statistically winning hand averages out to be 18 1/2, but you must forget that in this case, and stick to the 18. Why? There are only 3 cards that you have to worry about (the 2, 3, and 4) which could then set the dealer up on the next draw with a 19, 20 or 21. But even that is not much to worry about, as that is relying on a lot of chance for the house to pull that off. The house has to have one of those three cards underneath, and then pull one of the face cards or a nine just to beat you. You will still have the edge even if the dealer has the 10 or 11, because there will be six cards that can beat you, and six cards that will leave the dealer in either a losing or bad position, with one that leads to a push. But that is all only after he had the 3 or the 4 underneath in the first place! Sure it happens, but I guarantee you will do better standing on the soft 18 versus the dealers 7 or 8.

Finally, why stand on the soft 18, versus the dealer's ace? If you said because you can take insurance, you are absolutely WRONG. Dead wrong, and that's the sort of thinking that the casino wants you to have. They want you to be so afraid of the possible Blackjack that they, out of the kindness of their hearts will let you place an extra wager so that you can still keep your money. Yeah right, and they give everyone's money back at the end of the day too. It's a bad bet. I don't want to get into why insurance is so bad, I'll talk about that shortly, so I'll just say why you stand on the soft 18 vs. the dealer's ace. The chances of the dealer having Blackjack with the ace showing is only 31%. That's it, 31%. The remaining 69% of the time, the dealer will not have Blackjack. I know many of you right now are saying that's not possible, there are so many facecards, that the house must have a better chance then that. Okay, you do the math: 4 suits of 4, 10 value cards give the dealer the Blackjack. So that's 4x4= 16. Sixteen cards out of the standard 52 card deck give the dealer Blackjack when showing the ace. So that's 16/52, which gives you .30769. You then multiply that decimal by 100% to give you the value in percent, which gives you approximately 31%. That's all this game is about, mathematics and probability. So if you have a soft 18, while the dealer shows an ace, the chance of him having

Blackjack is only 31%. So, what else can beat you? The 8, and 9. Well, when taken together the chances of the dealer having an 8, 9, 10, J, Q, or King, and thus beating you is 46%. Not great, but that's still 54% in YOUR favor! Compare that to a 23% chance of taking a hit and getting a better hand. 54% vs. 23%. Which would you take? So that's why, on a soft 18 versus the dealer's ace, you stand, and take no insurance.

Memorize this, practice this at home. In fact don't even go to the casino until you can spout these figures from memory. It'll save you heartbreak and frustration, not to mention some cash.

3.8 DOUBLING DOWN: THE REAL MONEY MAKER IN BLACKJACK

That about sums up the ideas presented in this next section. This is one of the most important betting strategies involved in the game. When done properly, and under proper bankroll and money management conditions, this is the true advantage to the game. I hate seeing people screw up and not double down when they should. They're just throwing money away, and all for two reasons: lack of knowledge for the game and playing with a scared bankroll. These two together will eat you alive every time. But for those of you who are reading this, who want to learn, who want to win, and who will truly LISTEN, here are the times to do it.

The basic idea of doubling down, for those of you who are unfamiliar with the game, is to double the amount of your initial wager under certain circumstances, and hopefully win double what you normally would have. The problem is, many people do not know the appropriate time to double down, and will lose more often then they should. In these instances they are giving back to the casino a tremendous advantage, which is rightfully theirs. But there is a catch to this "favor" given by the casino: the player can only take one more card. That's it, so you better damn well know when to double down and when not to. The wrong times will kill you, the casinos know this and that's why they allow it. I can't count all of the times I've seen players double down on the wrong cards, or under the wrong situations. It's even worse to see players sitting with a strong doubling hand and not take advantage of this. In those cases, whether they win or lose, they're still giving money to the casino. They don't even realize it. They're just happy to have won the hand, and don't care they just let the casino keep the exact same amount that they won. You have to know when to double down. This is one aspect of the game that will really help to give the player, especially the non card-counter, the edge.

So, when do you do it? It's really very simple, and I guess that's what perplexes me when I see people making the wrong move. Look at the next table, memorize it, and once again don't even go near a casino until you've mastered it.

TABLE III: DOUBLE DOWN STRATEGIES

Player's Upcard	Dealer's Upcard									
Total	2	3	4	5	6	7	8	9	10-K	A
8	Hit	Hit	Hit	Db	Db	Hit	Hit	Hit	Hit	Hit
9	Hit	Db	Db	Db	Db	Hit	Hit	Hit	Hit	Hit
10	Db	Db	Db	Db	Db	Db	Db	Db	Hit	Hit
11	Db	Db	Db	Db	Db	Db	Db	Db	Db	Db

The scariest thing about these rules is probably the 8 vs. the dealer's 5 and 6. A lot of you will absolutely hate the idea of doubling down under these conditions, and it's easy to see why. So, what I am proposing is this: make this decision optional (unless of course you're a card-counter, and then you'll know almost exactly what to do). But decide what strategy you're gonna follow before you enter the casino, and stick to it. First, let's look at the pros and cons to each decision.

PRO: The odds of you getting a 2 or a 3 as your next card, which would put you at a good shot at drawing to a 20 or 21 is only 15.4%. Which means that 85.6% of the time you will draw a card that will leave you with a hand you would not hit against a dealer's 5 or 6 anyway. For example, if you pulled a 6, for a total of 14, you would not hit that against a dealer's 5 or 6 anyway. Also, the chances of the dealer having a bad hand, 12-

16 is 53 % with the 5 showing, and 61.5% when showing the 6. Either way the dealer is in a bad position.. Finally, the chance of you pulling a 17 or higher is 46.2%, not great, but when added to the poor odds for the dealer, you're sitting pretty.

CON: You're risking more with only a 31% chance of pulling an 18, and only a 7.7% chance of pulling a 19, a statistically winning hand (remember the 18 1/2 is the statistical goal in Blackjack). The dealer, while the chances are still slim, may still pull a good hand out of it, and you would then lose twice the amount on the double-down. Another problem is that you lose all chance of reaching 21, or even 20, because you are required to take only one card. As I pointed out before the odds are not great that you would end up in that position anyway, but it does happen.

Barring the 8 vs. the 5 and 6, which I'll allow as an option (though I do recommend doing it), the rest must be followed to the letter. This is a must.

One final thing I have to mention deals with a house Blackjack and how that affects your double down wager. When the dealer is showing an ace, the odds of him having the Blackjack is, as I mentioned earlier, 31%. But if he does have it, and you're playing in a casino where the dealer doesn't check his hole card, you still don't have to worry about losing your double down wager. This is because the casino will return your double wager back to you if the dealer has the Blackjack. So if you're sitting on an 11, and the dealer has an ace, you don't have to worry about losing twice your bet now because of a Blackjack, if he's got it, you get it back.

3.9 SPLITTING YOUR CARDS

This section of basic strategy deals with, you guessed it, pair splitting. For those of you who already know everything there is to know about splitting cards, congratulations, shut-up and keep reading. I can almost guarantee that you're still making mistakes and don't know as much as you think you do. You may be a regular dynamo, sitting on the floor of your living room with a deck of cards or a computer game, but this is real money we're talking about, during live action play, and this is one of the toughest parts to Blackjack. So if you really think you know it all, fine, you go back to playing with yourself on the floor (cards, that is) and I'll teach the rest of the readers how to win.

Splitting cards refers to playing two separate hands off of your initial two cards, because those two cards were a pair. For example, you were dealt two 8's for a total of 16. Instead of sitting on the worst hand in the casino, you have the option to split those two cards, and playing two separate hands. This is done by placing a chip amount equal to the sum of your original wager next to that original wager. The dealer will then deal to each of those cards as they are now separate hands. Sounds easy enough, right? Well, it is. Any dope can split a pair, but the hard part is knowing when to, and when not to do it. For example, you've been dealt two 8's, and the dealer is showing a 10. If you split these, you may end up with double 18s, with the dealer having a possible, 19, 20, or Blackjack. So, why risk twice the amount of money when the dealer may already beat you? Because the object is to win. Why take a hit on a definite 16, afraid to split against a POSSIBLE 19, 20, or 21? If you did that, you stand a 61.6% chance of breaking, for fear of the dealer already having 19, 20 or 21. (Which is only 46%) Not great, but still giving the player the advantage. The moral to this story: always, absolutely, positively beyond the shadow of a doubt split 8's. Against anything. You have a much better chance, statistically, of coming out ahead.

So what about the rest of the cards, you ask? Yes, they all have the same sort of rules like the 8's, and you will need to memorize exactly what to do in each scenario. It won't take too long, and it's really worth the time.

TABLE IV: BASIC STRATEGY - PAIR SPLITTING

Player's Upcard	Dealer's Upcard									
Total	2	3	4	5	6	7	8	9	10-K	A
2-2	Hit	Hit	Split	Split	Split	Split	Hit	Hit	Hit	Hit
3-3	Hit	Hit	Split	Split	Split	Split	Hit	Hit	Hit	Hit
6-6	Hit	Split	Split	Split	Split	Hit	Hit	Hit	Hit	Hit
7-7	Split	Split	Split	Split	Split	Split	Hit	Hit	Hit	Hit
8-8	Split	Split	Split	Split	Split	Split	Split	Split	Split	Split
9-9	Split	Split	Split	Split	Split	Split	Split	Split	Split	Split
A-A	Split	Split	Split	Split	Split	Split	Split	Split	Split	Split
Never split 4-4, 5-5, any 10's: follow previous rules.										

The table is not very difficult, but it will add a new dimension to your game once you have memorized it. There will never be any question in your mind of what to do. The decisions are already made, you just have to follow along.

A few quick notes that should be made after you've split the cards. From the above table it is clear that you must split all aces, as you could draw a total of 21 on both cards. I said 21, and not Blackjack, because when you split aces, they are not counted as Blackjack if you draw two 10's. Sorry, but that's the way it goes. Also, you should know that, unlike doubling down, when you split pairs, you are not required to stay on the next card. You may keep drawing to that hand just as if it were any other. So, for example, if you split 6-6, and on the first hand drew a 4, for a total of 10, you may then hit again. You do not have to stand on that card.

Before I continue, I'd like to briefly point out the "whys" to certain decisions in this table. For instance, why do you never split 10 value cards. (By the way, they don't have to be a pair in this instance: you COULD split a 10 and a queen or a jack and a king, or any combination of 10-K. But don't! The reason you don't split them is because you've already reached that magic number, 18 1/2, and now unless the dealer gets Blackjack or 21, you can not lose. I know some of you are thinking, "If the dealer is showing a six, why not split them, possibly get two more face cards, and let the dealer break. Then I'll win twice as much!" Sure, it will happen, sometimes, but not often enough to be worth the risk. Standing on a 20 wins about 85 % of the time, versus the dealer's 2-K upcard, and 69% of the time versus the dealer's ace, the chance of the player splitting a ten and drawing another 10 is still only 31%. If for some reason you do this, and you do pull two more face cards, you may have now taken the breaking cards for the dealer, the two consecutive face cards, and given the dealer a shot at making a good hand! It's a bad move, believe me, and if you do it you'll only show what a boob you are.

Never split 4-4 or 5-5, because when split, they leave you with a possible stiff hand, as opposed to a possible 18 or 19 for the 4-4, and 18-21 for the 5-5. You're just better off taking the card, or doubling down if the situation is right.

The reason you don't split 9's against a dealer's 7 is because he may already have the face underneath, and your 18 beats him. To be more specific, there is no one card the dealer could have that could beat you, and only one card that could cause a push. For instance, when showing a 7, if the dealer has a 10, J, Q or K, you automatically win. An ace will push. A 5, 6, 7, 8 or 9 leaves the dealer in a position to break. In fact, the only really threatening cards that the dealer could have is the 2, giving him a 9, a 3 giving him a 10, or a 4 giving him an 11, which will then put you in a position to lose with your 18. But bear in mind that the odds of the dealer having one of those three cards are a mere 23%, and then the dealer still has to pull the following:

Dealer's total on 2 cards:	Card needed to beat 18:	% Chance:
9	10, J, Q, K, A	38.5%
10	9, 10, J, Q, K, A	46.2%
11	8, 9, 10, J, Q, K, A	46.2%

In each of these cases, the chance of the dealer beating you is less than 50%. All things not being equal in a casino, I consider these odds half decent And remember, all this is IF the dealer is holding a 2, 3 or 4 underneath! So that's the logic behind not splitting 9-9 against a dealer's 7. Granted it's not flawless, and occasionally the dealer will win, but I believe this gives you the best chance of winning under those situations.

Now, I'm not asking you to memorize all of these percentages and reasons why you do what you do, I just want to explain where these ideas came from, and why you follow the tables. What I am asking, no TELLING, you to do is memorize the tables. It's not hard, and if you practice this at home, at work, or wherever, as long as it's not the casino, you'll eventually get it down perfectly. Because that's what you need to be. Perfect. Anything less than that's going to wind up costing you in the end.

Some of you more experienced players laugh at the warnings I'm giving about moves like those, but they happen every day. Not long ago, I watched a woman split a 20 versus a dealer's ace, take insurance, pull a 5 and a 7, stand on the 15, and watched as the dealer flipped over his card to reveal an 8, for a total of 19. The 20 she initially had would have won, but instead she lost her split and her insurance bet. And you know what? Not long after, she did it again, and even now she's probably still doing it. The worst part is, you can't correct that type of person. Try to give them any advice, and you usually wind up learning a whole new list of things you can do with your advice. Trust me, I've heard some doozies.

3.10 RESPLITTING: WHAT THE HELL DO I DO NOW?

At some point down the road, whether you go to the casino every day, or once a year, eventually this will happen to you. You'll split your pair, and WHAM! Up pops yet another of the same cards. So now you have to make a decision, do you split it again, just hit it, stand, or what?

First, think about this logically. If it were the correct move to split the exact same cards to begin with, how is that any different from now? It's not. You do the exact same thing, as before: you split the new pair.

Unfortunately, some casinos make the decision for you, and do not allow resplitting. Some of you may breathe a sigh of relief, but instead you should be swearing up a storm. Sure the decision has been taken away from you, and you don't have to put up a third bet (and sometimes even a fourth), but at the same time you're stuck with a lousy hand. One that either gives you a good shot at breaking or of being flat out beaten by the dealer if you don't take the hit. For example, suppose you are dealt a pair of 8s against a dealer's 2. You draw that 3rd 8, and now you're stuck with a sixteen, versus the dealers 2. While not an immediate loss, the dealer still has an advantage, even if he has the 12. Why? There are only four cards that can break him on the next draw, 10, J, Q, and K, and 5 (5, 6, 7, 8 and 9), that can beat your lousy 16. While not an outright slaughter, think of how much better off you'd be if you could have split the 3rd eight. So when given the opportunity, always resplit the hand.

3.11 DOUBLING AFTER THE SPLIT

I've talked about the importance of splitting cards, and the great advantage to the player when given the ability to double down. Now, it's time to combine the two: doubling down after the split. While it's not allowed in all casinos, its popularity is growing due to competition. God bless competition! When used properly, and by knowledgeable players, it can be a real asset.

Since you're not limited to receiving a single card after the split, as you are with doubling down, under the right conditions you can show a healthy profit for just one hand. For example, let's say you're dealt a pair of 8s. Logically, you'd split them, no matter what the dealer's upcard is. Now, say on the first split card, you're dealt a 3. For that hand you have a total of 11. So now, you double down. If you pull an 8-K, you're sitting pretty, with a 19-21, the range of statistically winning hands. Even if you did pull a "bad" card, A-7, you're still not in trouble yet, because you still have another hand to play, and the dealer may still break. And who knows, you may even be dealt another double down card on that next hand, and wind up really cleaning up.

So now the question is: when do I do it? That's easy. Since it's the same as playing two hands, the only thing you have to know is your basic strategy for doubling down. And I've already told you that, so it's nothing new. What is different, however, is your strategy for splitting when you're at a casino that allows doubling after the split. I must caution you that this strategy is just optional, and should only be used by aggressive players, who are already well ahead. The differences are:

1. On 2-2, 3-3, and 7-7 you split versus the dealer's 2-7.
2. On 4-4 you CAN split versus the dealer's 5-6.
3. On 6-6 split versus the dealer's 2-6.

Of all of these, the one I personally like the least is the 4-4 split. It can work versus the dealer's 5-6, because those are really poor cards for the dealer, and he has a good chance of breaking. So by splitting the fours, you're hoping to pick up on at least one of the hands a good double down card, such as a 5-7, and then cashing in on it. I don't like this option for the non-card counter, and if you're going to do it, I strongly suggest you learn card-counting. With card-counting, you know your chances of drawing the double card, or if you'll be stuck with a stiff hand.

The reason for splitting these hands is because the odds are that the dealer will break, and you will at least have doubled your profit, and maybe quadrupled it, for this hand. It doesn't always happen, and that one hand can take a small bankrolled player to the cleaners. But for the aggressive player, with a solid bankroll, this strategy can add a new dimension to your game, and I do recommend it, but with caution. It's not absolute, and if you really want to cash in on this strategy, learn advanced card counting.

3.12 INSURANCE: DON'T FALL FOR IT

How many of you routinely take insurance? Even if I don't count all of you who are lying about it, I'll wager it's still a whole hell of a lot of you. And that's a lot of money being handed back over to the casino, for a relatively bad bet. The genius that thought this one up did the casino one hell of a big favor.

For those of you who aren't familiar with the concept of insurance betting, it's simply a side bet during regular play that the dealer, when showing an ace, has blackjack. To make this wager, you simply place a bet above your cards in the area marked in nice big letters INSURANCE. The standard insurance bet is one half of your current wager on the hand. Since insurance pays 2:1, if you lose your hand but the dealer has Blackjack, you get double your insurance bet, which is equal to the total of your lost wager. For example, if you bet $10, and lost it to the dealer's Blackjack but had taken insurance for a total of $5, you would then break even on the hand, as the insurance wager would pay you $10. So basically you would win back the money you lost on your hand.

Sounds good right? The dealer has the almighty ace, and with all those face cards to contend with, you're better off protecting your wager. Wrong. No matter how tempting it is, it is simply a bad bet. The odds of the dealer having the Blackjack while showing the ace are about 31%. That means the other 69% of the time he won't have it, and you can say so long to your money. I know you're thinking it's not all that bad, because if you win the hand, and the dealer doesn't have Blackjack, you'll still take a profit. For example, if you wager $10 on the hand, and take insurance for $5. Let's say you win, as the dealer didn't have the 10 underneath. So what happens? You lose $5, but win $10 for a profit of $5. Doesn't sound too bad. But remember this: more than 2/3s of the time, the dealer will not have Blackjack, so for those times you definitely lose your insurance wager. So now, to keep from being slaughtered, you MUST win your normal wager every time, and that's pretty much an impossibility. So if you're losing your insurance bets 69% of the time, and DON'T win every time, you'll slowly get eaten alive.

Now, there are those of you who are just natural hedge betters, that is, people who want to reduce the amounts that you could lose. In craps, it's like playing the "Do not pass" line, while betting the point. If you seven out, you win your "Don't bet", lose your place bet, and take a small profit. If you make your point, you win your place bet, lose your "Don't bet", and take a small profit. (For those of you who are unfamiliar with craps, YES, this works.) So, either way you win, and when you lose you reduce those loses to the bare minimum. That's the thinking many people have about taking insurance. Well, I've got some news for you: it's a pseudo-hedge. Completely fake. You think you're protecting yourself, but instead, you're just leaving yourself wide open for a bigger loss. Unconvinced? If all the numbers and odds and statistics in the world won't convince you, (and if they don't, you're in the wrong game, my friends, because that's what Blackjack is, probability and statistics), then look at the casino. An old rule of thumb is: if the casino will let you do it, it's probably bad for you; if they WANT you to do it, it definitely is. So, obviously they want you to do it, otherwise they wouldn't write INSURANCE in big letters across the table, or have the dealers ASK the players for insurance every time they get an ace. You can bet your life that if the insurance bet paid more than 2:1, and gave the player an advantage, they'd never have it, much less ask you to do it!

The question is now, "Do I ever take insurance?" The answer is no. The average player should never take insurance. The only exception to the rules on insurance is for the card-counter. He can pretty much flip the odds to his favor, and fairly well know when to take the insurance. But even then, it's not guaranteed.

Some of you are still unconvinced, and will do it anyway. So, for those of you who won't listen to reason, I've taken the liberty of drawing up the few times when taking insurance may be slightly valid.

1. When you already have Blackjack: this is the only no lose bet for the player with insurance. If you have, say a $50 wager, and get Blackjack, you're sitting pretty. But if the dealer shows an ace and you don't want to take the chance of leaving that hand with no profit (even though that's only a 31% chance), here's what you do: take full, $25 insurance. That way, if the dealer has no Blackjack, you lose the $25, but get paid 3/2 on the Blackjack: $75. This leaves you with a $50 profit. If the dealer has Blackjack, your Blackjack is a push, so you don't

lose a dime on the hand wager, but get paid 2:1 on the insurance wager of $25, for a profit of $50. Not bad. Guaranteed profit.

2. If you have a higher than normal wager up, you might want to try to protect yourself. But be warned, you may very well lose both wagers, especially if you've been dealt a stiff hand (14, 15 or 16). I still suggest against it in this situation.

3. If you're at table and there are almost no 10 value cards out that round, and the dealer shows an ace, then there may be a slightly higher chance for the dealer to have the Blackjack, since there are little or no face cards currently out. This is called a TABLE COUNT, and it is a weak variation on the card-counting strategy.

4. Learn card-counting. You'll have a better understanding of the chances of the dealer having certain cards, and you'll give yourself the advantage when it comes to taking insurance.

Well, that about sums up insurance betting. Learn from what I've taught you, practice it at home. Count how many times the dealer has the Blackjack, and add up how much money you saved by not betting it. You'll be amazed.

3.13 SURRENDER: GOOD OR BAD?

Surrender. Some places have it, some don't. I'll bet that many of you are not at all familiar with what surrender is, much less when to do it. You're about to learn. Surrender is basically a way for the casino to take your money, without you putting up a fight. What they do is, allow you to quit the hand, if it's a bad one, pretend as if it was never dealt, and you're out of the hand. The catch is, it'll cost you 1/2 of your current bet. Let's say you've bet $5, and you're dealt a 16, while the dealer has a nine. You don't want to fight the dealer and draw to that card, when you just "know" a face card is coming. So you say "Surrender". The dealer will then scoop up your $5 chip, and replace it with a nice, shiny $2.50 chip. See what happened? This is the same as if you walked up to the table, gave the casino $2.50, and walked away without ever playing, because you were afraid the dealer MIGHT beat you. I've got news for you. Even when you're sitting on a 20, the dealer might beat you. If you're afraid of being beaten, so much so that you'll fold without a fight, you shouldn't be playing.

Despite this warning, there are times to do it, but those can be few and far between. If you really have to do it, the only times are:

1. Surrender on 15s and 16s against a dealer's 10-K.
2. Surrender on 16s also against a dealer's ace.

Any other times are a complete waste of your money, and just another example of the casino making a profit off a poorly skilled player.

4. BETTING STRATEGY

4.1 FIRST A LITTLE BIT OF ADVICE

In this section, I'm going to go into detail on a couple of the strategies that I utilize, and that you may want to incorporate into your own gambling style. These are suggested strategies, and you may alter them somewhat, but I would suggest that if you do so make it only slightly, and to the more conservative end, rather than the more liberal style.

But before I go into any of the strategies, I would first like to mention a key aspect to any system or strategy: table charting. Table charting is simply watching a particular table, usually for an extended period of time, to see how well that table is doing for the other players. Is the house winning consistently, or are the players really cleaning up? Does the table look "choppy", with a win here, and loss there? These are the questions that you must be able to answer before you even begin gambling. Don't just rush into the casino, and plop down a handful of cash at the first place that you see. Give it time, watch and see how well things are going. Remember, this is not just money you're playing with, but rent, vacations, Christmas presents, or whatever that money could (or should) buy.

I'll get into table charting in more detail later, but for now I wanted to just briefly state that no system or strategy can work, no matter how good it is, if you're at a bad table. By charting the tables, and not playing until you've seen a good one, you're increasing your chances of success drastically. Sure, it takes some self-control to do it and you might not have all of the time in the world, but I personally would rather watch a table for a few minutes and save myself a couple hundred dollars, then jump right in, give into the excitement, and walk off that table heartbroken and angry.

And now, on to betting strategies.

4.2 SYSTEM I: CLIMBING

This system is designed for the gamblers with the appropriate bankroll, that is 3 sessions of 40 times your initial bet. The steps to this strategy are as follows:

Chart the table. I would suggest watching the table for a trend in which the dealer is in a losing series. Once the dealer is in a trend for the player your first bet should $5. Once you win three consecutive hands, bump up your wager one unit, that is $5. You now have a $10 bet. If you win at the $10 level three consecutive times, up your bet to $15, and raise one unit now every 2nd consecutive win until you lose. When the loss comes, start over at $5. What this series looks like is:

$5, $5, $5, $10, $10, $10, $15, $15, $20, $20, $25, $25, $30.

If you reach the $30 betting series, you're in a really hot trend, especially if the dealer has broken more than 50% of the time, around 7 of the 13 hands. Now it is important to realize that the trend will not stay this way forever, in fact, with each successive winning hand it is more likely that the trend will end. So you have to stick to the following rule. If you lose ONCE, you start over at the $5 mark. That's it, just once. I don't care if you've made it only to the $15 series or the $50 series, once you lose once you start over. This will keep the casino from taking back most of the money that you just won.

Some of you are asking "Why start over again at the five dollar level when you're now already up a considerable sum of money?" After all, the higher you bet, the more you win right? Right. But, the other side of the coin is the higher you bet the more you can lose. Don't think you're a hot-shot just because the dealer lost the last 20 hands. The trend will turn, and if you insist on sitting at that table and betting higher amounts, you'll be cleaned out fast.

Suppose, for instance that you made it all the way to the $30 betting level. Now, you have won 13 hands for a total of $195. The next hand, you lose. You're now down to $165. Still, not bad by most standards. But what happens if you stick at that table betting $30? Disaster. It will take the casino only 7 wins to get back not only all of that money, but to put you $15 in the hole. Just 7. It took you 13 wins to get it, and they get it back, plus a profit, in only seven. And that's if you don't "chase". By chase, I mean continually raising your next bet to recoup a loss from the previous bet. For example, you just lost the $30 bet. You want that back, so your next bet is $60. If you lose that, your next bet is $120. If you lose that, BAM! You're in the hole $15 dollars. From up $195, to down $15 in three hands. You think that never happens? I've seen it just about every time I gamble. It is one of the best examples of a bad gambler, and it's incredibly common.

So what do you do? Break the bet all the way down to $5. If you lose 2 hands at the $5 level, pull back, and get out of the game. At that point you'll have a $155 profit for that trend. Wait for the next trend to surface, and when it does, jump in for another profit.

4.3 SYSTEM II: REGRESSION

This system entails a slightly different approach to betting, and it is my personal favorite. It's called the regression system.

The object of the regression system is to reduce the chances of the casino taking a large chunk of your winnings back, while allowing you to make a fairly consistent profit. It works like this:

Chart a table. When you've found one with a strong player trend, you wager 3 times the table minimum - no more, no less. After you win once, you reduce your bet down all the way to the table minimum. From then on you raise your bet every hand that you win, one unit, and pull back a profit. Once you lose, you start over at the beginning, with three times the table minimum.

This is a good system for those of you with the bankroll to do it, and can really show some good results.

4.4 SYSTEM III: DOUBLE REGRESSION

The double regression system follows exactly the same rules as the single regression, with one major difference. Once you've reached a predetermined number of hits, you reduce your bet all the way back down to the table minimum. That's right. Even in the middle of a winning series you reduce your bets. Personally, I wait until the $30 mark, but you can do it at other increments, within your bankroll. So how this looks, based on a $5 minimum table, is:

$15 wager

$5, take back a $10 profit

$10, take a $5 profit

$15, take a $10 profit

$20, take a $15 profit

$25 wager, take $20 profit

$30 wager, take $25 profit

$5 wager, start over

And so on. What's happening is, with each successive win, you're going up one unit, and taking back a profit. If at any point you lose a hand, you start over at $5. You don't have to start with the $15 wager because that was to give a quick lead during this series.

That begs the question, "Why start with a higher than minimum bet?" Here's the reason. Let's say you walk up to a table and bet the minimum of $5. You lose. On the next hand, you win. That's one loss and one win -- you're even. With this system, you're beginning with a higher than normal bet, to change the balance. Suppose you bet $15. You win. On the next hand you had bet $5 and lost. You then still have a net profit of $10! You now have options. You could:

1. Follow the regression system outlined above.
2. Bet $10 on you next bet, and if you lose still retain a $5 profit.
3. Bet the full $15, and try to double you winnings without risking any of your original bankroll.

Personally, I go with option number 1. It's more conservative, but it gives you a better chance of going home with a profit.

As great as this system sounds to many of you, it does have some major drawbacks. The biggest of which is the initial bet. A loss at that stage means you try again with another $15 bet. You lose that, and you're out $30 right there. By the way, that's where I call it quits at that table. I'll wait, or go chart another one. Sometimes, even if the trend looks really good, you lose anyway. But that's why it's called gambling.

For those of you who don't know how, card counting goes a long way in properly charting a table. These betting strategies work for the non-card counter, but if you just learn the basics of card counting, you will have a much better idea of the trend at the table, and could save you those $15 wagers quite often. I'd suggest you give it a shot.

Towards the end of the book I have included a basic section on card counting, so when you've finished that come back and re-read this section and see if you agree that card-counting will help you with these strategies.

4.5 SYSTEM IV: HIT AND RUN

This system does just what it says. Your objective is to take a lot of quick hits, and build up a profit gradually, without any one table eating you up. The method is simple. You begin, of course, by charting a table. When a good trend is apparent, you bet either double or triple the table minimum, for only one hit. That's it. You win, you walk. Find another table. Simple, huh?

Let's say you watch a table and the dealer has just busted, or lost 5 times in a row. You walk up, place a $15 bet, and if you win, you're up $15, and you find another table with another trend. After you're ahead about $150, you may, but it's not necessary, increase your wager to $20. It takes hours, and is extremely tedious, but you can pull some nice returns quite often.

4.6 SYSTEM V: SMALL BANKROLL BETTORS

That's right, I'm talking to you the small bettor, Mr. or Mrs. $100 bankroll. I know that despite my warnings, you'll still keep coming, endlessly looking for that big score. While I say that you should wait until you have the money to compete, many of you can't wait that long. So, for you I have a strategy that may prove profitable, but you probably won't like it.

The system is the same as the hit and run type with one exception: you're only betting $5. That's it. One $5 bet, and then you're gone, off to chart another table. This method takes time, and is the very definition of boring, but your objective is to win money, and with this controlled method of play, you will. It will never be the big score that you're looking for, but it just might give you the bankroll to try one of the other, more "exciting" methods.

4.7 SYSTEM VI: TREND BETTING

I've said it before and I'll say it again, if you want to win in a casino, you have to be in on the right trend. A trend is, as you should remember, nothing more than a detectable pattern of some occurrence. In Blackjack, a dealer might win ten times in a row. That's a trend highly in favor of the dealer. By the same token, you might be in a position where you win ten or more hands in a row. That's a trend in favor of the player. We've all seen someone at a table who seems like they "can't lose". They are, temporarily at best, in a good trend.

But trends are not just limited to ten wins here, ten wins there. A trend can be a win, loss, win, loss, etc. Just a series by which you can see a pattern. And it is precisely those patterns that we must look for when we gamble. Which, of course, brings me to the next betting strategy trend betting.

In trend betting, you begin as always, by charting a table, and waiting until the cards are set, or at least should be, and you are now in a better position to win then at other times. When that point comes, you jump in and wager higher than the table minimum, for this example we'll say that you're watching a $5 table. So you wager $15, three times the table minimum. On your first win, you go down one unit, or $5, so that you are now betting $10. If that wins, then jump up to a $15 dollar bet. On the next hit you go to $20, and continue going up $5 for each hand that you win. The initial drop in your wager is in case you lose the next hand, so that you would still show a $5 profit. Now if you did lose that second wager, you can do one of three things:

1. Drop down to a $5 bet
2. Do not bet on the next hand at all
3. Pull up and leave the table all together.

Each one of these has a valid rationale. For starters, let's examine choice number 3, leaving the table. If you leave now, you're up five dollars, and can go and find another table, perhaps one that you'll win more consecutive hands. It's a very conservative method, and you're not really betting with the trends, but who am I to argue with success? After all, a $5 win is still a success! In my opinion, however, you should stay in the game long enough to really gauge how the trend is going to go. If the reason you're leaving is because that $5 makes a difference in your bankroll, you have a shaky bankroll to begin with, and should re-assess your chosen method of play. The trend betting style, while appealing can take a huge chunk of your money, and if it doesn't favor you right off the bat, you'll be in trouble pretty damn quick! Try another method.

In case number two, sitting out for a few hands may help you to establish the trend at the table, without risking any more money. It's okay to sit out every once in a while but if it's because you don't have the right bankroll, then don't try this method. If it's because you have a "feeling" that the next hand is going to be bad, get up and leave the casino right now. Betting by your feelings is flat out just a bad way to gamble. I'd sooner play with a blindfold on then by my own misguided feelings. If you want to sit out a few hands to gauge whether or not the trend at this table is truly favorable, then this can be very beneficial, but be warned you may sit out on the winning hands!

Now let's look at case number three, reducing your bet down to $5. Okay, for the first hand, you won $15, but on the second hand, you lost $10. You still have a net profit of $5. That $5 is the total amount of money that you are willing to give back to the casino on the next hand. And if you do lose, you might want to consider leaving and charting a new table.

Why? Well, out of three hands you just played, you won one, but lost two, so you're only winning 33% of the time. With that figure, you won't be in the game for too much longer before it starts to eat you up. But here's the good news: you won one out of three, and yet you still aren't any worse off then when you sat down! You won one, the casino won two, and yet you're still even. Even better you can see that the current trend is working towards the casino 66% of the time.

Granted the trend is not completely evident, as it could change at any moment, but don't waste your time messing around with a trend that "could change". Wait for the one that you win 2, 3 or even more hands right off the bat. It will keep your losses down and you in the game longer. And the longer you're in the game, the more chance you'll have of hitting the good, long trend.

But back to that $5. As I said, that's your stake for this table. If you lose it, you're done. If you win, the tables are reversed, and you're now winning 66% of the time. You've won 2 and lost 1, for a net profit of $10. Not bad. After you've won that first hand, you're either going to be up zero if you lose the next two, or up $10 if you win one more. And that's how this trend betting is played. You bet in intervals of three hands and see how the trend is developing. So your next wager should be $15. And at this point you're already up $10 so if you lose the first hand of the new series you're only down $5, and that's if you lose that 1st hand.

In a nutshell, this strategy looks like this:

1. 1st bet $15.
2. If you win, your second bet is $10.
3. If that hits, you're in a fairly good trend, so you go up to $15, and raise $5 each hand until you lose, and then you start at $15 again.
4. If you lose your second wager, the $10 bet, you bet the last $5 of your profit.
5. If you lose the $5, you're done for that table, the trend has been revealed, and you're not down one penny.
6. If you win the $5 wager, you're now up $10, and the trend looks to be fairly decent, so you start a new round at $15, and follow that trend in the same fashion.

By utilizing this strategy, you're setting a smaller, more attainable goal, while at the same time making the trend more readily apparent. Each of your wagers is determined by the outcome of the previous hands, and you can figure out how often you are winning. All in all, it's a pretty good system.

4.8 PLAYING MULTIPLE HANDS

Maybe you've seen it. Maybe you've done it. Or maybe you wonder if YOU should do it. The "it" I'm referring to is playing multiple hands at once. (I'm not talking about the "game" Multiple Hand Blackjack, just playing multiple hands at a regular table.)

Unlike Blackjack, some casino games do not allow you to play more than one hand at a time, such as Caribbean Stud poker, or Let it Ride. But in Blackjack, you do have the option of playing more than one hand. Should you do this? Statistically, it makes very little difference. The major determining factor is your bankroll. Playing more than one hand, while it can win you a lot of money, it can very quickly eat away at even a decent sized bankroll. Personally, I never play more than one hand at a table. I just don't like the "feeling" that I'm competing with myself.

If you insist on playing multiple hands, there are some guidelines that you should follow. For starters, you sure as hell better be a card counter. Just watching the table and following the trend is too risky when wagering on two hands. Secondly, your bankroll must be 40 times the minimum wager for each hand that you play. So if you play 2 spots, at $5 each, your bankroll should be $400. That's a pretty large bankroll, but that's the minimum you need if you insist on playing this way.

4.9 THE MARTINGALE SYSTEM

Many of you have heard of this system, some know it by name, others do not. It was developed years ago and guarantees that if you follow it to the letter, you will be a winner. In some sense it is true. If you do follow it 100%, yes, you are guaranteed to be a winner. The catch is that it is impossible to follow it to the letter in a casino.

What this system revolves around is the idea that, in any given series, you will eventually win. For example, you may lose 10, 15, even 20 hands of Blackjack in a row, but if you keep playing, you will eventually win. So, what you're supposed to do is after every loss, you double your previous bet. If you bet $5, and lose, your next bet is $10. If that loses, the next is $20, and so on. Yes, you will eventually win, but in a casino that is an impossible strategy. Why? Because the casino has self-control. Let's continue with the progression, and see what I mean. Okay, you lose the $20, so bet $40. Then $80, next is $160, then $320, and then $640. But wait a minute. The table limit is only $500, so you can't bet $640. So, you've lost a total of only 7 hands, it cost you $620, and there is no way you can bet high enough on the next hand to win. You're screwed.

The other basic problem with this system is the amount of money you would need to play. Suppose the table did have a higher maximum bet? You'd need thousands of dollars just to play a few more hands, a sum which most of you don't readily have.

This system is a no-no. Theoretically, sure it's great, you win ever time. But in real life, in the casino, it's a downright impossibility. Never, ever use this system.

4.10 CARD-COUNTING FOR BEGINNERS

Is it difficult? The answer is a simple, resounding NO! The secret to card counting rests in being able to accurately label the cards that come out as either a +1, or a -1, and then watch until an advantage appears. For example, watch as the cards are dealt, and mentally list all higher cards of a ten value or higher (10, J, Q, K or Ace) as a +1, and at the same time label all of the lower value cards, (2, 3, 4, 5 and 6) as -1. The rest, (7, 8 and 9) are considered a wash, as the dealer will rest with the same statistical advantage of drawing these cards as the player. In other words, for each time the dealer pulls these cards, you should have them with the same frequency. So, just don't count them. Many people prefer to label the cards numerically just the opposite, making lower value cards the +1, and the higher value as -1. It really doesn't make a difference, it just depends on your preference.

Let's say that you're standing by a table, watching, not playing, and counting the cards as they come out. There are five people sitting at this table playing. The cards that come out are as follows: 2, 5, 2, 3, K, 6, 5, Q, 9. Now if you were to count this, the value would be, a negative four. Six low valued countable cards, two higher valued countable cards (K and Q) and one non-counted card, the nine. Roughly translated, there are now four more low cards out of this deck than there are high cards. Keep watching this deal until there is an even higher negative value, roughly between 35 and 45. Why do you do this? To put it simply, let's just restate the object of the game: to reach 21 or be closer to 21 than the dealer, without going over. By counting cards, you can tell a good percentage of the time what cards to expect both you and the dealer to receive. In other words, let's say that you are watching the table for a few hours (that's right, I said a few HOURS), and the count is now at about a negative 45. Red flags should start flashing all around you, as there are now 45 more low, garbage cards out than there are face cards. Almost the size of one full deck! (Remember that many casinos, especially those in Atlantic City, use six and eight deck shoes) That means that the remaining decks are now "loaded" with face cards. And the higher the negative value, the more face cards there are. So how is this information helpful? Well, now you have a markedly increased chance of pulling a "winning" hand, which is statistically about

18 1/2. With a highly negative shoe, you have a good chance of being dealt a 20 or Blackjack right off the bat, without worrying about whether or not you should take a hit, stick, or whether or not the next card will break you. That's the time to bet, and not a moment before. When the ratio of low cards to high cards is high, you give yourself a better chance of winning.

Now, some people absolutely balk at the idea of waiting around, watching the tables for hours, counting away until the cards are just right. They say things like "I came to play, not to watch," or "Standing around is so boring, I'll just play a little bit." How can people be so ridiculous as to think that it is better to go to a casino, jump on the first table they find, and lose all of the money that they came with, then it is to go home a winner. Because that is the object of gambling: to win, not to play. If you wanna play, go buy a baseball, it will save you plenty of money in the long run. If you want to win, then memorize basic strategy and the basic card counting. As I have already shown you, the method is not difficult, the hardest point is in staying focused and developing patience.

Let's go back to our example. Okay, you're watching the table and you have just reached a negative value of 45. Now is the time to sit down, and jump in on the next hand. Hopefully you will draw a money hand, a nineteen, twenty or Blackjack, and the dealer will pull either a lower hand, the same hand (a push that I consider a much better alternative to losing) or be sitting on a 12-16. Granted the dealer still has the ability to pull a good card while they have a 12-16 and possibly beating you (unless, of course you have Blackjack), but given the still high negative value, the dealer is much more likely to break, that is exceed twenty-one. That is one very good reason to card count: to know when to play, and when to quit. So what's next? Well, even during the hand that you just sat in on, you counted the cards as they came out of the shoe, and everybody had either a 20 or Blackjack. So now what do you do? Regardless of whether you won, lost or pushed, the negative value has now fallen below the minimum required to give the player a strong advantage while playing, so now you have options.

Option One: Leave the table. Pull up all of your money, step back and watch some more, either at that table or go and find another. The key is to secure a profit, no matter how small. A win, is a win, is a win.... You then wait until the cards show a high negative value and begin the procedure again. I know, it's a grind, a long dragged out why-the-hell-am-I-doing-this grind. I'll tell you why: to win. To give yourself the best possible ammunition against the casino, to leave with more money than you started with. That's why.

Option Two: Stay at the table, betting the absolute table minimum until the cards show a strong trend in the negative value once again. There are pluses and minuses to this strategy, but the advantage to this system over others is that it allows you to get in on the action of the tables, rather than standing around, possibly for hours, while waiting for the cards to develop a definite, mathematical trend. In this instance, the card-counting is especially important, not only to know when to bet in higher increments, but also to know beyond the basic hitting/standing strategy. In other words, your knowledge of the point count can lead you to make mathematically sound decisions as to whether or not to take a hit or stand on your current value. For example, if you have a two card total of 13, while the dealer is showing a 7, you might want to consider not taking a hit, even with a thirteen, and hope that the dealer's down card is a nine or less, when your counted value is a fairly high negative value, like a

25. The likelihood is that the next card is a face card that will break you, so by deferring that card to the dealer, you set the house up to break, IF THAT CARD IS A 9 OR LOWER. Now of course you don't have an incredible chance of succeeding because the dealer might have a total of seventeen already, as the point count is decidedly negative, or the dealer might have a total of 10 or 11, and the next face card could give the house a 20, or twenty one. But remember, while you allowed the dealer to pull a great hand by not taking the next card, you would have lost anyway by pulling that face card! Also, remember that while the count is decidedly negative, at 20-25, the value is not so incredibly negative that it is definite that the dealer will have a decent hand with his down card. Now the higher the negative value becomes, the more likelihood there is to the dealer having a good hand, so this works the best with an average negative value of about 17-25. Any higher and you start getting into the realm of a good negative value, where most of the upcoming cards are face cards.

Now, also remember during this method of play there is the possibility of the lower value cards continuing to come, which could result in a loss for the player because the dealer pulled a series of lower valued cards (2-6) that gave him a decent hand, while you stood on a lower value of cards, like the 13. So what defense is there to this? There are two important aspects to this dilemma. One, the dealer, when pulling into that series of low cards still has the possibility of breaking, with either just the low cards, a mixture of low and face cards, or by simply pulling the wash cards, the 7, 8 or 9. Two, as the dealer pulls this series of lower valued cards, the total count value becomes negative and the higher the probability that your next hand will be a winning hand, like a 20 or Blackjack. Yes, there is a chance of losing and you may lose the $5 wager, but your next wager could yield you a larger return than the previous loss.

5. SELF-CONTROL

5.1 SELF-CONTROL AND MONEY MANAGEMENT

So far, I have told you when to hit or stand, depending on the probability of success. Now, I'm going to teach you how to bet. Most people have a random style to their betting, a habit that you must break. You need many things to be a successful gambler, and having self-control and money management rank right up towards the top.

So what do I mean when I say money management? I mean a planned, premeditated strategy, a method of attack that is unchanging. If you decide to raise your bet only after the dealer has lost five consecutive hands, then do that. But ONLY after the dealer has lost five consecutive hands. Don't think for a minute that you have the right to change your pattern, because you don't. Get into the habit of treating every hand, every dollar in a particular method. Don't raise or lower your bets based on a feeling. Sure it may work some of the time, but in the long run, the casino will clean up on your "feeling."

In this next section, we're going to get into how you should manage your money while gambling, when you should pull back, and when you should play on. It entails a system by which you set for yourself a goal and a limit to the amount of money that will change hands between the casino and yourself.

5.2 SELF-CONTROL: THE FOUNDATION OF WINNING

One of the largest determining factors as to whether or not you are going to win in a casino (I'm not even going to comment about whether or not you should be there in the first place) is self-discipline. Without it, you don't stand a chance in hell of walking out of that casino with a profit. I know, some of you are fondly recalling the time you turned $50 in $500, or thinking that luck plays a large part in the life of the gambler, but think again. That one-time-win does not balance out all of the times you have lost, and the times ahead that are sure to come. Luck plays no part in gambling, only skill. The casinos NEVER rely on luck, so why should you? They let the vigorish and the ignorance of the average gambler work for them to produce a tidy profit. You think those million dollar chandeliers were just donated to the casino? They came from your sweat and tears, from your wallets, and the wallets of everyone else that fails to master a game before they play. From those who have no self-control.

How do you get self-control? You cram it down your throat. You weigh the plusses and minuses; you do anything possible to get it, because if you don't you might as well just have your paychecks mailed to the casino. At least that will save you money on gas!

So what is self-control in a casino? Simply put, it is the ability to:

1. Set a specific amount that you want to win, that is easily attainable by your bankroll.
2. Set a definite amount that you will allow yourself to lose - about 50% of your total bankroll.
3. Be prepared to walk, or better yet, RUN, when you reach either of these.

That is the beginning of discipline. Sure there are other things, such as not playing until the trend is right, knowing when to increase/reduce your bets, and knowing never, ever to chase. (Chase refers to betting higher and higher amounts after loses, hoping to recapture your losses. This spells almost certain disaster). But since we've already covered those areas, we're going to stick with learning how to control your bankroll.

5.3 BETTING AND SELF-CONTROL

All wagering in a casino is governed by certain rules. There are table minimums, in Atlantic City, NJ for example, these are never lower than $5. There are table maximums, ranging from $500 and up. What does this mean? Well, the casinos, even with the vigorish, and the knowledge that their profit for the day is secured by the sheer number of poor gambler that come in every hour, have discipline. They set limits. You wanna play? Bet at least $5. You're in a winning streak, you can't bet more than the table maximum. The casino sets limits on how much profit they will allow you to take when in that hot streak. Sure, you can ask the pit boss to raise the maximum for you, and they might. But by and large, you will be confined within those limits. Self-control. The casinos thrive on its own self-control, and believe me, they'll wait out your streak, until your poor gambling technique starts to shine through, and return to them a profit.

So, if the casinos can thrive on self-control, why can't the player? They can, and must, if they hope to walk out of there with more wins than losses. How do you do it? Rule number 1: Set a specific amount that you want to win, based on your BANKROLL, and make sure that amount is easily attainable. Personally, I would suggest about 10-30% of you original bankroll. This figure is more conservative than your standard professional gambler, who may advocate upwards of 50%. I know that to many of you, either of these figures are too small and not the type of win you are looking for. For example, if your total bankroll is $100, then you should expect to win, and be happy with, $10. Well, who the hell is happy with that? You should be. Believe me, a $10 win is much better than a $100 loss. Do you want to win more money? Then you better bring more money. The theory is basically this: when you walk into a casino, is it fairly easy to win $10? Yes, it is. That's 10%. By taking that same 10%, with a higher bankroll, the payoff gets better. You win $100 with a thousand-dollar bankroll, $150 with $1500, and so forth. Or you could allow yourself to take a 15% profit, and increase that even more. As I said, I'm more conservative with the amounts that I want to win, but that's only because I want to win! I LOVE the feeling of leaving a casino up money, no matter how small. Just as long as it's not a loss. This strategy is important for two reasons:

1. It will give you a better chance of leaving the casino with a profit, and
2. During the occasional times when the cards are particularly in your favor, a good streak, you may walk out of the casino winning well over the 30% that I am advocating.

Being a small, but consistent winner is a hell of a lot better than being a large and consistent loser! And believe me, the big scores will come, but until then, the smaller scores will add up.

One final note in all of this is that you can set your own win percentages, as long as they are easily attainable, and you are comfortable with them. Remember that just because you reach that percentage doesn't mean that you stop playing, as you would miss most of the streaks that you need. Rather use this percentage as a baseline win percentage, the absolute minimum you want to leave with. For example, let's say that you reach the total percentage value that you wanted, about $150 dollars. Your next step should not be to leave (unless of course the table is now decidedly cold, or in a highly positive count). Rather you should break off about 30%-50% of the total profit, and continue to wager with that amount, while the bulk of the profit goes back in the pocket, along with the original bankroll. So in this instance, you take 30% of the $150, which is $45, and continue wagering with that at either this or another table. But remember, just because you are ahead, don't fall into a sudden fit of philanthropy, and lose all of the 30%! Use the same self-control that you had when you won the original $150, and try to turn a profit from your NEW starting bankroll, the $45. By the way, don't be afraid to add that $45 (or what's left of it) back into the winnings pile whenever you want to, just make sure it's when you are leaving. You are never, ever, never to go back into the 70% winnings pile, no matter how much you "feel" the next shoe is going to be good, or if you want "just one more hand". It will eat you up every time.

Another important aspect of self-control that will make a difference in your approach to gambling (and to your winnings) is the idea of setting forth a particular dollar amount by which you will not give to the casino, or a loss limit. This figure is based on your starting bankroll, and should be the absolute limit to the amount of money that you will lose. Do not ever go beyond this number. It should always be decided upon beforehand, and once play has begun, it should never be changed. I personally use a standard 50% limit for two reasons: 1) so that I still have at least half of what I started with and it will be easier to rebuild that same starting bankroll for the next trip, and 2) so that the amount lost doesn't "kill" you on that long ride home. (And I don't care if you live five minutes up the road from a casino, when you lose it's STILL a long ride home!!!)

The final aspect of self-control in gambling that I will discuss is when to increase/decrease you bet. Stated simply, you never increase your wagers during a losing session, only when you are soundly in a trend in which you are winning. Now this changes slightly once you have mastered the subtle trick of card counting, but the idea is sound. Only for the expert card counter does raising your bet during a losing session come into play, because he knows, within reason, the type of cards that are about to appear during a shoe. Any other time and you are committing gambler's suicide by raising your wagers.

5.4 THE IMPORTANCE OF CHARTING A TABLE

I see it ever day I enter a casino, car loads, busloads, singles, couples, self-proclaimed professionals, just about everybody going into a casino, rushing up to any table, any game (as long as it's the $5, or, lower table). If they go to play craps, and it's packed, they hop on Blackjack, or Let it Ride, or Caribbean Stud poker, or, for God's sake, even the Big Wheel. They don't care what they bet on as long as there's a chance to gamble. And they lose. They get more money, run right back up to the tables, and crash headlong into disaster. I have personally stood there and watched while the same person takes the only available seat at a table, lose all their money, get more and lose it again, repeat the process twice more, and grumble about how rotten their luck is. And that is not the exception to the rule, but the average gambler! The following is a list of four of the biggest mistakes made by both new and seasoned gamblers.

1. No self-control
2. No set strategy

3. Poor play due to the lack of knowledge of the game. You have got to be perfect to stand a chance against the casino. No mistakes. This is not an impossibility. All that it takes is a little time, a little memorization (I have included the charts with the basics of what you must do on each hand.), and a strong desire to win. Remember this is not a teddy bear you're trying to win at a local fairground, it's cash, car payments, vacations, and all the other things that money can buy. Whether it's money you've saved, stolen or previously won, it's the reason you're at the casino and no other.

4. Did not chart the table. What do I mean by charting the table? Watch it. See the trends that go on before your eyes. Count the cards as they come out, without risking a single nickel. Wait. When the trend turns and the cards are coming out strongly in the favor of the player, that's when you play. This is the only time in the casino when the power is truly yours: before you start playing. The house has to deal constantly, to anyone who sits down, even when the trend is strongly towards the player. They cannot say "this table is doing to well, we're going to shut it down. You'll have to go over to one of those other tables." Could you imagine if they

did? There would be rioting. (But I can guarantee you that a fairly large number of gamblers would march right on over, without a second thought!) But no, they don't do that. They realize that the trends will eventually change, and the poor betting abilities of most players will still return a profit to the house. And believe me, they're right. But by charting, you're taking some of the power away from the casino. You're saying, "I'm gonna bet only when the cards will work for me, not you." And the house is powerless to stop you. They'll continue dealing to the saps who just run right up and throw their money away, while you wait for an advantage. Be patient, it'll come. It really will.

That is what charting is all about. Watching tables as if waiting for the cards to say, "I'm ready to be nice now," and of course, you'll oblige them. Test it. Just once. Next time you go into a casino, chose a table and watch how many people just walk up and sit down without so much as a glance at the trend. The dealer might have just pulled four Blackjacks in a row, and won the last 27 hands, and people will still sit down. Worse yet, there are people who have been there for hours, are down $700-800, and are still there, most of whom barely know basic strategy, and even less who know how to card count.

5.5 GO HOME WITH A PROFIT: ANY PROFIT!

That says it all. Any day, any time that you can leave the casino with a profit, be it $5 dollars or $5000, it's a win, and you've already done better than over 80% of all the people who entered into the casino that day. How do you do this? Self-control, betting strategies, predetermined amounts, a proper bankroll, and easily reached goals. That's how to leave with a profit. Sound simple? It's not. It takes a lot of control to walk away from a table after only 3 hands, and after watching it for 2 hours. It takes a lot of control to be able to reduce your bets and increase them at the right times. It takes a lot of control to turn around and walk away for the day, knowing that you still have at least 50% of your bankroll in your pocket. And sometimes, it really hurts. But believe me, it hurts more when you're kicking yourself because you should have left only down $150, instead of $300. (Usually more because of credit cards, bank cards or cash advances.) It'll happen. And those of you who don't listen, it'll keep on happening until you get smart, learn control, and learn how to win.

5.6 WHEN TO WALK, WHEN TO RUN

So, you've come this far, you know basic strategy and the basics of card counting. The next question is: when do I walk from a table? There are about as many different views about this as there are gamblers, and the best answer is -- it depends. You have to answer certain questions about your particular method of play, before rushing in with an answer to that. Some of the all time worst are:

1. When I lose all of my money.
2. When the shoe turns real bad.
3. After 3-5 consecutive losses.

or my personal favorite,

4. I had a feeling.

Number four, in my opinion is the worst possible type of gambler, a superstitious player. These are the people who bet, play and leave based on their own misguided intuition or superstition. I don't know, maybe you're right with your guesses 100% of the time, or that you truly are psychic and know that the dealer is going to win the next 237 consecutive hands, and then it would be all right. But let me ask you this, if you've got that kind of power, why do you have to make money gambling here in the first place?

No, the only determining factor to when you should leave the table is what type of player are you. Are you a Type I: hit and run, Type II: active counter, or Type III: passive counter. Now of course there are other variations on the same theme, but these will be, largely, the bulk of the card-counters.

In Type I betting, as you already know, the object is to watch a table until the trend is in the favor of the player, at a predetermined negative card value, and then play a predetermined number of hands beginning with bets above the table minimum, and then reducing them as the sequential hands become more positive in value (that is, more in favor of the house). When you have then reduced your bets down to the table minimum (depending at what your starting figure was), a type I player will be done, probably for that shoe or longer, until the count is once again in your favor.

This of course is no guarantee of a win, because the dealer still has the likelihood of pulling a good hand as well (but remember, with each player that is dealt face cards, with no lower valued cards, the dealer has that less a chance of being dealt a "good hand". But by and large your chance to win is greatly increased by knowing the point value of the cards before you begin playing. Now this type of player can go for a long time, and indeed it might take a long time before he/she even has a chance to sit! But you must always keep in mind that no strategy is guaranteed, only your chances are increased. So make sure you have a predetermined profit goal before you start your wagering. Once you reach this, you're either finished with the table, and perhaps the day, or you may decide to play further (once the point is in your favor again), but this time with only a percentage of your winnings. In my opinion, once you reach your goal, the day should be over, as counting takes a lot of concentration, as well as time, and the last thing that you want to do is give an advantage back to the house because you're tired and your concentration falters. It can happen!

A Type II player, the active counter, will sit at a table (after the initial charting) making the larger bets at first, then reducing them, and playing at the table minimum and raising slightly to coincide with favorable points. The higher the negative value the higher the bet (but don't go crazy: you still have to play a controlled game, based on the point count), but never to exceed or equal the original wager. Why? If the reason you sat at the table was because the point count was so good, don't risk giving back to the casino the money that you won in the first place, unless of course the point value is the same or higher. Generally, with this method, you rely on the current count, table count and basic strategy. This type of player usually gets more action then the hit and run type, but a particularly bad shoe, or trends toward the dealer, can eat away at any profits faster than you would think! My suggestion with this type of player is to set a situational specific loss limit, based on your current win/loss ratio. If you won the first few hands at higher increments, lets say you picked up a quick $200. This is your first table; you're above your win goal for this table by $50. I personally suggest, in this situation, you alter your initial loss limit to suit the situation, one that is in favor of the player. So now you readjust your loss limit to 40% of the $50, or $20. What this means is that you still have $20 to work with, while taking an excess profit of $30, above your original win goal. You just always want to take at least a 60% profit above your excess, whenever you get the chance. Remember, as a card counter, you know the chance of being dealt a favorable hand when the point is low, so in my opinion you should not bet. But if you're at a marginal table, and you've already taken a profit as I have described, this system protects the bulk of your excess profit. Finally, when that excess profit is gone, don't walk, run!!!

The third type of player for this method is the passive counter. As you know a passive counter follows the same premises of the type II counter, except they never increase their bet until the point value is re-established to the original level it was when he/she originally began. Using the strategies and counting techniques this player can usually remain fairly constant in a win to loss ratio, unless a dealer-orientated trend begins to occur. In this instance, I would suggest taking a loss of the excess or predetermined profit (if you have not reached the excess level already) of only 20% of the current profit. For example, if your win goal is $150, and you've currently won $100, but the shoe is favorable towards the dealer, when you lose $20 that's it for the table. If your knowledge of the point value, and count strategy can't break the dealer's streak, you maximize your remaining profit margin in this way. So when you fall back to having an $80, pull back and wait for a new trend and point value.

Remember that these are just suggestions for when to finish your betting at a table. You can play with the ideas, and come up with one that's more comfortable for you, but remember: YOU HAVE TO STOP WHEN THE POINT AND TREND IS AGAINST YOU! You must set limits to how much of your winnings you will give back to the casino, and the lower the percentage you give them the better.

6. PROBABILITY AND TRENDS

6.1 PROBABILITY AND YOU

Ah, good old probability. To some, probability is an old enemy, to others, a good friend. (A very lonely friend, I'd wager.) Way back in the beginning of the book, ages ago it seems, I gave you a brief glimpse about the importance of understanding probability in gambling. I tried to make it sound as easy as possible, but some of you still don't believe that probability plays an important role in the life of a gambler. Tough crap. Accept it or lose, it's your choice.

For a gambler, knowing the chances of an outcome being favorable or unfavorable is as important as breathing, because you can restrict yourself to the type of games that you will play. A fifty-fifty shot is a hell of a lot better bet than a forty-to-one. Sure it doesn't pay as much, but once you understand trends you can grind out a good profit quite often.

In the section on basic strategy, of included some of the percentages for particular things to happen. You don't have to memorize these percentages, but you should realize that they represent the chances for a card to appear, under those circumstances. That knowledge helps you to make the best possible decisions during play and this will, in turn, increase your profits.

6.2 DISPELLING THE MYTH OF LUCK

Luck is a term that you hear in casinos more than any other word. (But that's probably only because people pray silently!) "My luck is rotten today," or "Look at that guy's chips, he's on a lucky roll!", are just a couple of the expressions frequently spouted by the average gambler. But whether you believe me or not, luck really has nothing, (or at least shouldn't) to do with it. Gambling is nothing more than a series of occurrences based on probability and statistics. The way to win is to play only those games that offer the best chance of winning.

To further increase those odds, you have to follow the best, most mathematically sound systems and strategies. By doing this, you take away most of the "chance" in games. And that's an ideal situation for making money through gambling. Oh, sure, it won't always work, because there's no way to predict definitively what will happen next. But through probability, trends, and strategy, you can sure as hell narrow down the possible outcomes. That will leave you sitting with pretty good odds in the long run.

So the next time you're tempted to blame your bad luck on the outcome of the day, stop and think of all of the mistakes you made first. How many 30-1 shots did you bet on? How many really big scores did you go for, and lose? These are the reasons you got wiped out. Your bad gaming methods will always shine through, and wind up costing you a bundle.

6.3 THE WINNING STREAK

No matter what anybody ever tells you, and I don't care who they are, trends do occur. The people who don't accept that, just can't see the big picture. I'd also wager that most of those who do believe in the theory of trends don't truly know why.

So, what are trends? I've devoted a lot of time in this book referring to the effects of trends on outcome, and how they are used in gambling, but I haven't really discussed what they are. Simply put, a trend is a series of events that occur in a specific, detectable pattern. For example, how many of you have been at a Blackjack table, and watched as the dealer won 15 hands in a row? I have, and I've seen it many times, and sometimes they go even longer than that. I've also seen the dealer break in series like that. It happens, and that series is called a trend.

In craps, people sometimes shoot for hours (personally the longest I've ever seen was 3) and win incredible sums of money, all because the trend was working for them. Yet, I've still heard over and over again that there is no such thing as a trend. The common example is flipping a coin. If you flip a coin, what are the odds that it will be heads? Answer 50%. If you flip it again, what are the odds? You're right, 50%. And again, and again, and again. All 50 %. Each time it landed on heads, and each individual throw was a fifty - fifty chance right? Right. So then there is no trend, because they were all fifty-fifty. Wrong. Take a step farther back and look at what has happened. You just flipped that coin 10 times, and each time, it landed on heads. Sure, each individual random occurrence was a 50-50 shot, but what are the chances of throwing those 10 heads in a row? 50-50? No way. So the trend in that situation was towards heads. The thrower beat the 50-50 odds of each individual throw, and drove down those odds by doing it 10 times. So the trend starts to take shape. Now, take one more step back. By the laws of probability, that action, that is throwing 10 heads in a row, must eventually occur. In other words, the laws of probability themselves suggest that trends, such as throwing 10 heads in a row, must occur. And that is exactly what is happening in a casino. At some point in a 50-50 game, one side, or the other will win more often. The odds only balance out and become 50-50 in the long run.

So, by using this knowledge of trends, a gambler with a keen eye, strong strategy, and excellent betting habits can utilize the trend. You must bear in mind, however, that all things are still governed by probability, and the trend will eventually shift to the opposite. And to detect this you must first realize that this is exactly what happens.

Hence, you can see the importance of charting a table. You want to be in on the hot trends, and by utilizing the betting strategies that are contained in this book, you can reduce the losses when the trend turns.

I have a very simple name for this system.

I call it winning.

7. PATIENCE

7.1 PATIENCE IS A VIRTUE

Not only is patience a virtue, but when it comes to gambling, it is a downright necessity. Up until now, I've hammered you with strategy, money management, self-control, and a variety of other aspects of gambling, some of which you were already familiar with. Now, I'd like to just say a few words on the importance of patience.

Patience and self-control go hand in hand, especially in gambling. Self-control is the ability to handle your bankroll properly; patience is handling your emotions properly. Without patience in a casino, your money is as good as theirs.

So, when do you need patience? When you're charting a table, when you're in a losing streak and you're tempted to increase your bet in order to recoup your loses quickly, when you just get off the bus and when you only have a few hours to play. Those are the times you need patience. In fact, from the time you walk into a casino, to the time you walk out, you better not rush one damn thing, not one, or you'll be up the creek.

How many times have you seen people rush up to the first table they can gamble at, without so much as a glance at the trend? How many times have you done it? Countless times, I'm sure. But you have to stop it. There is no need to rush. I know you may only have a short break or only a few hours to go and you need to get your gambling fix before time is up, but more often then not, your impatience will cost you big. Maybe even your entire bankroll. Is it really worth it?

So, here's what I want you to do to get into the habit of exercising patience when in a casino. The next time you go, I want you circle around the tables of the game you've decided to play no less then twice, and I mean *walk,* don't jog, don't run, just a nice, comfortable gait. And after those two laps you will hopefully have calmed down enough to begin your work of charting the tables. The idea is to try to acclimate yourself to the casino environment. It may sound silly, especially to you veterans, but even you must admit how your pulse begins to race as you enter the casino. The excitement mounts, and for many of you, self-control will go right out the window. You have to force yourself to relax and become accustomed to the casino. This is not a waste of time. This method will teach you patience, until such a time as you are able to walk in yourself, and calmly begin to examine the trends at all of the tables, without sitting down right away just to satisfy your need to gamble. It will work.

Don't underestimate the power of patience. It is one of the key elements to being a successful gambler, and it is no less important than strategy or bankroll. Without patience, your strategy is compromised, and your bankroll goes right out the window. Get used to waiting, or get used to the agony of the drive home at the end of the trip.

7.2 PATIENCE AND THE CASINO

On any given day that you enter the casino, the majority of the people that you see will leave losing. That's a fact, and there's nothing you or anyone else can do to change that. But what is that the case? After all, in a game of chance, doesn't the casino run the same risk of losing as you do?

Not quite. If you really think about it, the casino has the advantage over you on so many levels, that you might want to consider bagging the whole idea of gambling, and take up an easier hobby, like theoretical physics.

Okay, okay, it's not quite that bad, but look at just some of the ways the casino automatically has an edge on you:

1. Bankroll. No ifs, ands, or buts, the casino has the money to just run you into the ground. In fact, that's one of the major reasons why the casino can secure itself a daily profit. The casino knows that most people are poor gamblers, and that many are flat out beginners who don't know a thing about the games that they are playing. And with a seemingly endless bankroll, the casino will just flat out wear your bankroll down - until there's nothing left.

2. Vigorish. I mentioned earlier what exactly the vigorish is, so those of you who READ that section should be fairly familiar with what it is. For those of you who don't remember it's the edge that the casino has in its favor on any given game. There is no escaping it, and the longer you stay in a casino the more the vigorish will eat you up. It may take a while, but eventually, you'll be leaving with nothing.

3. Rules. Everything done in the casino, by the casino has to follow certain rules. The dealer must stand on a 17, but hit on 16. A player can not touch the cards in Blackjack. Blackjack pays 3 to 2. These are all rules that you and the casino must abide by. So why is this an advantage to the casino? Because you get to make decisions. You are the one to decide whether to stay, or take a hit. You have to know when to double down, or when to surrender. They do not. If they have a 16, they have to take a hit. You do not. They have rules that they have to follow.

Most people who gamble do not set rules for themselves, and that's a big reason why they lose. You **NEED** to set rules for yourself, a strategy that you must follow. That strategy, in this case, is basic strategy. Basic strategy is nothing more than a series of dos and don'ts. It's the rules you need to follow in order to gamble successfully.

4. Patience. They've got it, most of you don't. They can wear you down, and wait you out, until you finally give in and make yet another deposit into the casino bank. And for most, the wait is not very long. You need patience. You need to be able control your urges to play, and starting building the urge to win, consistently. And to do that, you've gotta have patience.

These are just some of the reasons why the casino has the edge on you, and some of them you can change. Take back some of the edge that they have. It will make a big difference in your wallet.

8. EVERYTHING ELSE YOU NEED TO KNOW IN A CASINO

8.1 CASINO COMPS

Comps. To some people these become an obsession. A comp, or complimentary, is a gift. A free-be, that usually takes the form of a meal, like a lunch or dinner, tickets to one of the casino's shows, and sometimes even a room. Usually, these gifts go to the people that the casino wants to keep coming back, like the big bettors, the real high-rollers.

So, how do you get these comps. Bet high. That's the only way, and unless you can afford it, and would have bet that way anyway, I would not suggest doing it. But you would be surprised at how many people with short bankrolls throw away dollar after dollar in an attempt to get these freebies.

Why is it so important to these people that they get comped? Is it just a need to be recognized, or do they just feel that they're entitled to the same treatment as the high-rollers? I've seen people sit down at a table, buy in for about $150, and within 20 minutes of $5 betting, they are asking for a free lunch. Honestly now, do you really think they deserve it?

The pit boss knows what your betting habits are, almost right from the initial buy-in, and those little amounts that most people bring to a table do not justify a free anything. Yet routinely, the pit boss is subjected to downright begging from many players for a free meal. And when the pit boss politely rejects them, you'd think they were just stabbed by their best friend. Immediately the anger wells up in their faces, and you know they're thinking of taking their business elsewhere, to a place where they'll be treated with the respect they deserve. Well, I've got news for you people. That's not going to be in a casino. You're not the king of the castle unless you bet like it. And if you don't have the right bankroll, you'll lose your throne pretty quick.

Places like Atlantic City, New Jersey have, I think, spoiled the average player. There is a constant stream of cocktail waitresses, providing free drinks for the customers, and to some people this has become a requirement, and not just a courtesy. Sure the casino's have reasons for doing this, like keeping players at a table even during the worst of trends, but this is a courtesy just the same.

How do they keep you at the table? Well, let's suppose you're playing at a table, and the waitress comes by and takes your order. During the following interim, the trend on the table becomes progressively worse. Yet, instead of leaving, you continue to plunk down more and more money, just because you know that your drink is on the way. They're eating him alive, and yet he stays where he is because his drink is on the way and he figures that the casino owes him one. By the time the waitress comes back, he's dropped another $60, making that one of the most expensive drinks in history.

One notion I would like to dispel right now deals with ulterior motives for the free drinks. Some people actually believe that the casinos offer these drinks for the sole purpose of getting their patrons intoxicated, so that they'll be at a big disadvantage while playing, and play badly. I've got news for you folks, I've seen how some people play when sober, and for many of them, their moves couldn't get much worse. The casinos do not have to try to get you drunk in order to take your money. Besides that, there's no rule requiring you to have a drink when you play. If you're afraid of becoming drunk, then don't drink alcohol. Order a soda, or a coffee, or anything that your heart desires, just don't blame the casino for your intoxication. That's all your fault.

Personally, I do not drink while in the casino. At most, I'll have a cup of coffee. I am just not fond of the thought of being in less than 100% control. I need to think quickly and clearly because every decision I make must be flawless. You might want to consider that.

8.2 TIPPING

Though you may not realize it, there are a couple of times, while in the casino, it would be a good idea to tip. I know many of you feel that tipping in the casino is a waste, and that you shouldn't bother since you've already given them enough of your hard-earned dough. Should you tip? In my opinion, yes. I know that may have turned off a lot of you, but I have some pretty valid reasons for my thinking.

For one, let's consider the waitresses. Why tip her? Because it's courteous, for starters. This girl is running around constantly, taking hundreds of order, and they usually return within a reasonable length of time. So what do you have? You've gotten a free drink, someone to make it for you, and someone to bring it right to you, while you can continue to bet. You don't have to go thirsty, and you don't have to leave your seat, which can be a real asset during those hot trends. So why not just fork over a dollar, and be grateful? That's it. Just one stinking miserable dollar, and you get all that service. You're paying more just to have a guy put a couple cards in your face, so why not give $1 to the waitress who actually brings you something?

The other time you should tip is when you have a particularly friendly dealer, and the trend in the table is going well for you. Let's say that you've just picked up a few hundred dollars through a couple of great shoes, and the dealer has been very polite, friendly, and maybe even helpful, what's wrong with dropping him a couple of bucks? They don't make all that much money, and a good part of their salary revolves around the tips, or tokes. Now I'm not saying to tip constantly, or when you have a quiet, moody dealer, but if you get a nice one, show your appreciation.

How do you tip at the table? There are two methods for tipping the dealers:

1. Drop it on the table in front of him. He will usually then thank you, and announce to the pit boss that he was just tipped. The money is then placed in a tip box on the side of the dealer.

2. Place a bet for him. This is the one that I suggest. It makes the dealer feel as if he's a part of the action. To do this, you simply place the amount of the tip slightly above your wager, and when the hand is played, if you win, the dealer pays you, and the tip amount. Once everybody is paid, the dealer then collects the original tip, as well as the payout. So, if you

win the dealer is getting twice the amount of your original tip. The money once again goes into the tip box.

There are other reasons for tipping the dealer besides courtesy. Though many of you don't believe, and you really can't prove it, the dealers will treat the tippers a little better than the other, quiet people at the table. They may give suggestions for what to do on certain hands, or just be more talkative to you in general.

They also have a slight tendency to "forget" to take certain losing wagers from the tippers. For example, if the dealer pulled a 19, but you had an 18, he may "miscount" and pay you for what was a losing hand. You think I'm nuts? Try it sometime. It happens a lot.

8.3 ETIQUETTE IN THE CASINO

For many of you reading this book, a casino is a new, and often frightening place. It's filled with people, noise, security guards, and a general hodgepodge of activity. Some of you first timers, (and a lot of you regulars) need to know a little bit about casino etiquette.

All of the casino personnel can spot a person with class in an instant. That's primarily because most of the denizens of the gambling community have little or no class in a casino. They carry themselves very poorly. In fact, the dealers, pit bosses, floor people, and anybody else working in the casino can tell in a minute if you're a beginner, a bad player, a smart player, or have a scared bankroll.

If you need help in the casino, or want to color in your chips or anything, do it in a respectful manner. Nothing is more annoying then having to take orders from a loudmouthed jerk, and believe me if you're one of them, half the casino is rooting against you. Be as polite and courteous to people as you would like them to be to you.

While playing Blackjack, here are some tips that you should follow:

1. Don't just throw your money down in the middle of a hand. Wait until the hand is over, or even the shoe, before getting chips.
2. Chart the table before sitting down.
3. After you've received your money, thank the dealer.
4. Don't space everything out: your chips, the ashtray, your drinks. Leave some room at the table for everyone else!
5. Don't badger people about what you think was a bad move. You may be wrong yourself.
6. Don't beg for comps from the pit boss.
7. Place your bets up on time: don't make the dealer have to remind you to place your bet every five minutes.
8. Don't scream and yell if you lose, or gloat if you win.
9. Don't blame the dealer for winning. He's not playing against you, the house is.
10. Don't touch the cards.

These are some basic rules of etiquette that you should follow. I know some of you feel that since you're betting your money that entitles you to act however you want, but show a little respect for others. Remember, every second you're at a table, you're being watched. The pit boss may think twice about comping a loudmouthed jerk.

8.4 SECURITY AT THE CASINO

Whether you know this or not, each move you make in a casino is being watched. This is accomplished by a system called the casino eye, a series of video cameras covering every table, and every move that the dealers and players make. This is for both your protection and the casinos. Since you are constantly being watched, you have less of a chance of people stealing from you (which, by the way, does happen), and the casino is protected from cheaters.

Security guards are also constantly walking around the casino, and are ready to respond to any trouble. They are usually very helpful people, and if you're lost, or need assistance, they're there to help. Don't be afraid to ask them anything.

Unfortunately, even with all of the security cameras and personnel, you must still be on your guard in the casino. The thieves who frequent the casinos are real pros, and they rarely work alone. Since they can't just outright mug you, they have developed craftier ways of taking what's yours. I've listed some of the major ones.

1. At the slot machines, most of the thieves work in groups of two or three, and they usually target those people with

large amounts of coin kept in separate buckets. What usually happens is, the thieves will throw a coin at the leg of the target. That person will usually turn, and either pick up the coin, or stop to ask the next closest person if it is theirs. While the target is preoccupied, another of the group then moves by quickly, and snatches one of the unattended buckets. When a third person is involved, the thieves will then hand off the bucket to that person, who is walking in an opposite direction. By the time the victim turns around, or notices what has happened, the thieves are long since gone. And so is the money.

2. Other, less organized thieves will target a woman's purse, or just steal a handful of coins out of the slot bin, when it is filled. These people use pretty much the same style, they distract their intended victim, but are more like "hit and run" thieves, and are not usually as skilled.

At the table, the thieves usually select targets that are either older, have a large stack of chips, and are not paying particularly close attention to their winnings. For these people the thieves usually:

1. Take the seat next to their victim, usually with a small amount of chips, and pretend to play. While play is continuing, they

steal some of their neighbor's chips by reaching over with the hand to the opposite side of the victim. In other words, they block your line of vision with their right arm and shoulder, while stealing your money with their left.

2. Other thieves will stand behind you, and when you're not looking, or concentrating on the cards, reach under you to your stack of chips, and steal a little at a time. Usually, by the time you notice you're short a few chips, they are already at another table, selecting a new victim.

So how can you combat these criminals. The easiest way is to not be picked as a target. In other words, count your chips frequently, or keep them in an inaccessible pocket, or at least one that a thief could not unnoticeably steal from. At the slot machines, cash in your coins frequently, or at least don't keep separate buckets of chips away from your body. Don't look away from your money for too long, and be wary of any sudden movements, talkative or distracting people. It could be a set-up.

8.5 PLAYER INTIMIDATION

Casinos intimidate many of you. That's understandable. It can be a scary, hostile place, and friends can quickly become enemies. For these reasons, and many others, people when they do gamble, tend to do it poorly. It starts with lack of knowledge for the games, lack of strategy, and lack of self-control, but continues, and indeed in augments by fear. Many people are so intimidated by the table games, for example, that they confine themselves to playing slot machines, or only certain table games, like the Big Wheel. These games, while fun, give the house a big advantage against the player, and that is indeed most prevalent with the slot machines. For those of you who don't believe me, then answer me this: why is the largest money maker in the casino the slot machine?

Many people are just absolutely terrified at the idea of having to actually sit with other people, or have to work with a dealer, and would more readily hand over their money to a casino by playing games that have a higher vigorish. They are controlled by fear.

Another reason some people are intimidated at the tables is because of the other players. Often I have heard people screaming at other players for making certain moves, whether they were bad or good. These people may be right, and they may be wrong, but regardless they will defend their viewpoint to the death. (And I'll bet you they'll die poor.) These people can really intimidate you, especially if you're a beginner. My advice is, to learn all of the right moves. What will happen then is you'll win more often and you'll know you're in the right if another player tries to tell you you're wrong.

8.6 THE ULTIMATE GOAL IN GAMBLING: WINNING

Why do you gamble? Do you gamble to pass the time? To have fun? To show off to your friends? No. You gamble because of money. You want it, you need it, and you simply have to have it to survive. But in order to get that money, you have to know how to win. As I've said before, the amounts are not the important thing. It's simply the win. Would you rather win $10, or lose $300? Not much of a decision is it. But if you go into a casino, will all of these master plans of breaking the bank, winning thousands, if not millions, chances are very great that you'll come out a loser. But if you go in with a logical, attainable goal, based on bankroll, backed with skill, you'll be a winner. And that is, after all, the ultimate goal in gambling.

8.7 LET'S WRAP IT UP.

There you have it, the basics of Blackjack, with a little taste of card-counting. After you've learned everything contained in this book, and it won't be in one night, you'll be on the road to success in gambling. No one can win 100% of the time, so don't get discouraged if your first try ends up as a loss. Take that experience, and learn from it. Examine what you did right, and what you did wrong. Re-read the book, and see if you missed anything. In my opinion before every venture into a casino, you should brush up on the charts, to make sure you have everything down perfectly. In the casino, you have to be perfect.

COMING SOON: The Basics of Craps

A RavenHaus Publishing Book

New Jersey

COMING SOON: *The Basics of Craps*

By the author of ***BlackJack: The Real Deal***, J. Phillip Vogel, ***The Basics of Craps*** is the second in the series of books showing you how to beat the casinos at their own games.

_____ BlackJack: The Real Deal 0-9659845-0-8 $14.95

_____ The Basics of Craps $14.95

Name ______________________________

Address ______________________________

City ____________________ State_______ Zip _________

Please send me the RavenHaus Publishing Company books I've checked above.

I am enclosing $______________

plus

Postage & handling* $______________

Sales Tax (where applicable) $______________

Total amount enclosed $______________

*Add $4 for the first book and $1 for each additional book.

Send check or money order (no cash or CODs) to:
RavenHaus Publishing Company Mail Sales, 2 Fox Hill Rd.,
Califon, NJ 97830

Prices and numbers subject to change without notice.
Valid in the U.S. only.
All orders subject to availability.